BRITISH STEAM
SINCE 1900

A high proportion of famous engines are covered in this absorbing and controversial book – the great *Pacifics* of Gresley, Stanier, and Bulleid, the GWR *Castles* and *Kings*, Churchward's earlier GWR designs, the Midland Compounds, and many others.

In addition there is a clear description of the various parts of the steam locomotive, their functions and operation, supported by diagrams and excellent illustrations of representative locomotive types.

'A very good guide' *Railway Modeller*

'Intensely readable and provocative ... the knowledgeable enthusiast will find himself alternately applauding and arguing hotly with the author.'
Country Life

Also available in the David & Charles Series

The David & Charles Series

BRITISH STEAM SINCE 1900

W. A. TUPLIN
D Sc, MI Mech E

UNABRIDGED

PAN BOOKS LTD : LONDON

First published 1969 by David & Charles (Publishers) Ltd.
This edition published 1971 by Pan Books Ltd.,
33 Tothill Street, London, S.W.1

ISBN 0 330 02721 2

2nd Printing 1971

© W. A. Tuplin, 1969

Printed in Great Britain by
Cox & Wyman Ltd, London, Reading and Fakenham

CONTENTS

ILLUSTRATIONS IN PHOTOGRAVURE

(between pages 84 and 85)

Duchess of Montrose taking the LMS 'Mid-day Scot'
northward past South Kenton
(By courtesy of Mr C. R. L. Coles)

LINE DRAWINGS

PREFACE

This book was written primarily for the amateur student and the enthusiastic admirer of the steam locomotive rather than for the professional locomotive engineer. It has been made possible by many years of observation of locomotives and railway working from the outside, by study of the voluminous literature, by knowledge gained from conversations with railwaymen, and from journeys, mostly illicit, on engines in service.

In recent years some revelations by retired railwaymen of what went on behind the scenes in design, construction and operation of railway locomotives are barely credible by the man-in-the-street but not surprising to those acquainted with the incongruities in any large technical organization. Uncompromising adherence to old practices regardless of the known existence of far superior ones is not peculiar to railway work and it would be idle to pretend that it never existed. At the other extreme, unashamed utilization of what was succeeding elsewhere took Great Western locomotive practice very nearly to the ultimate ideal in one step, some twenty-five years ahead of the rest of Great Britain.

On most British railways the chief mechanical engineer was responsible for design of the locomotives and it is traditional to attach his name to those designed whilst he was in charge. This does not necessarily mean, however, that he did any of the designing himself, as he had many other things to do. Some CMEs took an active part in design, while others lacked time or ability to do so; every CME had to rely largely on technical staff to produce workable designs and drawings. Elsewhere in the organization were men who made engines and men who made them go. Communication and cooperation between the three groups was not ideal on every railway.

The efforts of a score of design staffs of different railways, independently feeling their ways to what was essentially a common goal, produced designs in profusion to the delight of any interested observer who was not at the same time a railway shareholder.

The full story could well occupy half a dozen books and might be summarized in half a dozen pages. Any intermediate length provides such difficulties for the author as to leave him as thoroughly dissatisfied as discerning authors usually are. Here the normal difficulties in deciding what to miss out and in what way to present the remainder are intensified by the size of the subject and the multiplicity of its facets. The author's only refuge from his doubts as to whether he has found the best way of doing what he has attempted is the reflection that the identity of the best way is largely a matter of opinion.

ACKNOWLEDGEMENTS

The Bibliography (p 196) represents only a minute fraction of the extent to which the author is indebted to published work on railway subjects. He is also indebted to many railway-men for word-of-mouth information too enlightening for anyone to dare to publish directly; use of it has forbidden acceptance of some details of conventionally recorded history.

Most of the illustrations are reproduced from photographs made available by the courtesy of British Railways and others mentioned elsewhere.

REFERENCE LETTERS FOR VARIOUS RAILWAYS

BR – British Railways (from nationalization in 1948)
CR – Caledonian
FR – Furness (LMS)
GC – Great Central
GE – Great Eastern
GN – Great Northern
GNS – Great North of Scotland
GS – Glasgow & South Western
GSW – Great Southern & Western (Ireland)
GW – Great Western – also Great Western group (formed in 1923)
HR – Highland (LMS)
LBS – London Brighton & South Coast
LMS – London Midland & Scottish (group formed in 1923)
LNE – London & North Eastern (group formed in 1923)
LNW – London & North Western
LSW – London & South Western
LTS – London Tilbury & Southend
LY – Lancashire & Yorkshire
Met – Metropolitan
MR – Midland
NE – North Eastern
NS – North Stafford (LMS)
SD – Somerset & Dorset (LMS)
SE – South Eastern & Chatham
SR – Southern (group formed in 1923)

WHEEL ARRANGEMENT AND CYLINDER ARRANGEMENT

This book uses the conventional Whyte system of denoting the wheel arrangement but adds a prefix giving the number of cylinders:

> 2 means two outside cylinders and no others
> 3 means two outside cylinders and one inside
> 4 means two outside cylinders and two inside

Absence of a prefix means two inside cylinders and no others. Addition of C to the prefix implies compound expansion.

> T means an engine with side-tanks
> ST means an engine with a saddle tank
> PT means an engine with pannier tanks
> WT means an engine with a well-tank.

Other notation

Bib. draws attention to the reference number of the relevant item in the Bibliography on p 196.

R draws attention to the reference number of the relevant item in the tables beginning on p 172.

A implies double chimney (Fig 10A).

K implies Kylchap double exhaust (Fig 10B).

L implies Lemaître exhaust (Fig 10C).

CHAPTER ONE

INTRODUCTORY

AN ACCOUNT of the development of the British steam locomotive since 1900 could be completed by a short dissertation
on superheating, a few remarks on piston valves and a note on
Walschaerts valve gear, for, apart from these, there was very
little change in broad principle after 1900 or indeed after
1830. By good judgement, and perhaps some luck, George
Stephenson combined in the *Planet* the multi-tubular boiler,
horizontal cylinders, and draught induced by exhaust steam
and no superior substitute for these essentials has ever been
found in spite of prodigies of ingenuity and effort. By 1832
excellent piston valves had been designed (and some were in
use in stationary engines) and by 1852 superheating had been
tried. These last two features did not achieve practical success in locomotives until just after the year 1900 and then, in
principle, the steam locomotive was as good as ever it
could be. Later developments were only in size and in detail
improvements that reduced running costs. If the locomotive
engineers of Great Britain (to cast the net no further) had got
together from 1900 to 1905, and if some stupendous genius
could have inspired them to truly cooperative effort on
rational lines, design could have been finalized with very
great economy all round at the cost of some dismay for the
amateur enthusiast who likes to see plenty of variety.

Instead, there were at any one time a score of locomotive
engineers all doing what was essentially the same job, each in
his own different way and each, in greater or lesser degree,
influenced by the human failings of pride, self-righteousness,
adherence to tradition, deliberate blindness to virtue elsewhere, and reluctance to believe that anyone else's job was

quite so difficult as his own. The result was most gratifying
to the many people who, under the emotional spell of the
steam locomotive, found delight in examining its numerous
variations. Many of them were needless, from any broad
viewpoint, many of them quite irrational, but what a galaxy
of shining, multi-coloured, coal-consuming, dirt-producing
locomotive engines did the railways of Britain exhibit to the
fascinated amateur!

The steam locomotive was, by modern technological
standards at least, a very simple piece of machinery. The
mechanism was quite straightforward; the boiler worked in
rather violent conditions but the basic thermodynamical
principles behind it were well understood by 1850 and study
of steam-flow through the engine offered no special difficulties. Yet there is ample evidence that even with the twentieth
century a quarter spent, there were eminent locomotive
engineers who did not in fact appreciate certain elementary
points in basic design, and an expert in all the branches of
basic design, detail design, construction, operation, and
maintenance was a rarity.

What, then, made it possible for success to be achieved by
locomotives that in some features of design at least were not
so good as they might have been? Firstly, the fact that under
the spur of pride or of fear of disfavour, enginemen could
find ways of getting much more out of an engine than normal
handling would produce and so even a bad design might be
made to work well enough. Secondly, the fact that there was
little or no interchange of operating information between
different railways, so that a locomotive that was regarded
with satisfaction on one line might have been severely
criticized on another. It is certain that two of the very few
'locomotive exchanges' between different companies had a
very marked and immediate effect; one case, at least, revealed
a lamentable failure to appreciate a basically important point
in design.

The suggestion that a bit of clear thinking in 1900 to 1905

could have saved a lot of designers' efforts in the following half-century may inspire the reader to remark that it is easy enough now to say what people should have done sixty years ago. This, on the face of it, is a valid comment, but it is cancelled by the fact that someone actually did the clear thinking at that time. This was G. J. Churchward, in charge of the Great Western locomotive department, and the lime-light accorded to some other locomotive engineers in later years should not be allowed to hide the fact that this was the man who showed the way. He did it, not by any supernatural genius but just by plain 'horse-sense', that rare characteristic that would solve most of our problems if it became wide-spread. All that he did was to realize that, by 1900, every variation in the conventional steam locomotive had been tried out by somebody somewhere or other and that, if he made the best use of the knowledge acquired from all this vast experience, he might expect to take the design of steam locomotives about as far as it could ever go. He knew that to make full use of existing knowledge is the first step in any sensible development. Everyone else admits it too, if cross-examined, but most people fail to do it simply because it is easier to think up one's own solution of a problem than to do a library research that reveals that someone had solved it fifty years ago in a manner more elegant than one could imagine.

In the nineteenth century, Great Western locomotives were not typical British locomotives; in the twentieth century, their style changed completely and they were still not typical British locomotives. In writing of development in the twentieth century one cannot help remarking that Great Western practice leapt ahead in the first five years, kept its lead for the next twenty, and, having advanced about as far as possible, was gradually overtaken and caught by the time nationalization of the railways took place. After that the Churchward procedure was applied again, and the British Railways standard designs were evolved after study of all the

relevant information possessed by the four groups. The
resulting locomotives offended some conventional aesthetic
sensibilities, just as those of Churchward had done, and their
only real difference from his was their incorporation of
Walschaerts valve gear. This type of valve gear (shown in
Fig 4) had not been widely accepted in America when Churchward was producing his basic standards; otherwise he would
most probably have adopted it.

Many features in the development of British steam locomotives from 1910 onwards were inferior to what Great
Western practice was already demonstrating, and such
failures to make use of existing knowledge may be regarded as
causes for criticism. On the other hand, had everyone adopted
the best known procedure in design there would have been
much less to write about in reviewing the last half-century of
British steam. But only on the appearance of the first British
Railways standard design of locomotive in 1951 had ultimate
rationalization of British design procedure taken shape and
by then the end of steam was not far off. For the enthusiastic
student of the steam locomotive in Britain, variety was
maintained almost to the end. Very soon after common-
sense gained full control, the subject died.

Until the diesel locomotive was clearly becoming accepted
in North America, little effort was made in Britain to design
steam locomotives with the object of minimizing the time
and cost of daily labour in preventing the locomotive from
being choked by dirt. The firebox and ashpan had to be
emptied, half-burnt coal had to be taken from the smokebox,
the firetubes had to be cleared of soot, and their firebox ends
had to be cleared of rings of built-up slag. Oil-boxes had to be
refilled daily or more frequently. Every week or so, the boiler
had to be emptied and the sludge and scale removed as
thoroughly as possible by water jets and rods with scraper
ends inserted through holes from which the 'washout-plugs'
had been removed. It took several hours to raise a boiler
from cold to full steam pressure. Every steam locomotive

was the field of an endless battle against internal dirt, and the latest advances in design were made to assist maintenance staff in that battle.

In general, regular maintenance work on steam locomotives was done in spite of appalling difficulties most of which could have been markedly reduced by changes in detail design. On many railways the gulf between drawing-office and running-shed was such that complaints did not usually travel from the latter to the former and such as did were treated with scant concern.

One could find, for example, an inside cylinder fed with oil by a pipe that could not be reconnected after coming loose without lifting the boiler out of the engine. A complete list of twentieth-century British atrocities of this kind would run into hundreds and would grimly exemplify both man's stupid inhumanity to man and man's equally stupid acceptance of it. Very severe criticism could properly be directed not so much at the original mistake but at failure to correct it in a machine with a life expectation of thirty years.

BASIC ELEMENTS

No review of the development of any machine has any real meaning to a reader who is doubtful how the machine is supposed to work. So at some danger to the patience of those readers who are clear on the subject (and many extraordinary misunderstandings persist about it) a brief review is given here in conjunction with Fig 1.

First of all, the steam locomotive was a vehicle constrained to follow rails by wheels with flanges that lay between the rails. Each pair of wheels was fixed to a steel axle (7) up to about 10 ins in diameter and each axle took part of the locomotive's weight transmitted through two axleboxes (8) and two springs (9). ('Axlebox' is the locomotive engineer's name for what engineers in general call a 'bearing'.) When

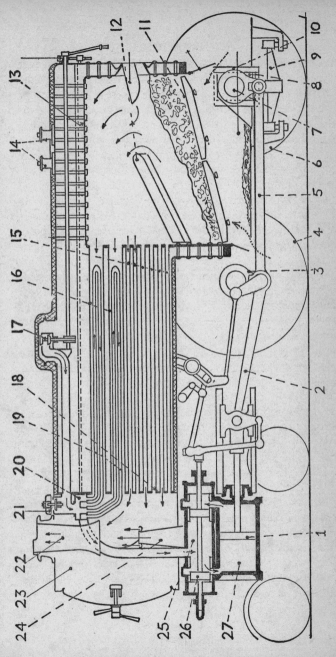

1. Section of typical locomotive

the engine ran over any irregularity in the track, the springs yielded a little and the axleboxes slid up and down in guides (10) called 'hornblocks'. In order to keep this up-and-down movement within reasonable limits the springs had to be quite stiff, and by riding on certain locomotives one might be led to imagine that they had no springs at all.

In a completed locomotive, the axleboxes were almost invisible unless they were applied outside the wheels as was nearly always the case for the axles under the tender and usually for non-driving rear wheels of the engine itself. In locomotives with double frames (few remained in service so late as 1950) all the axles had axleboxes outside the wheels, and crank axles usually had inside axleboxes in addition to those outside.

Steam pressure on pistons (1) acting through piston rods and connecting-rods (2) and cranks (3) caused rotation of the associated wheels which, by virtue of friction with the rails at the points of contact, thereupon urged the locomotive along the track and were consequently called 'driving wheels' (4). The driving effort was usually shared with other wheels (6) connected to the driving wheels by coupling-rods (5) and such wheels were called 'coupled wheels'. (The term 'driving wheels' was sometimes used for the combination of driving wheels and coupled wheels.) Such wheels were normally allowed no perceptible side movement in relation to the frame of the engine, although such lateral freedom did develop as the result of wear of the axleboxes and of their guides. The distance between the first and last axles of a set of driving wheels and coupled wheels was the 'rigid wheelbase'.

A locomotive had to have at least two cylinders, working cranks at right angles, for otherwise it might stop with the cranks in such positions of unfavourable leverage that even full steam pressure in the cylinders would fail to re-start the train.

A two-cylinder engine might have the cylinders either 'outside' (as on Stephenson's *Rocket* and eg, Fig 1) the

connecting-rods, urging crankpins fixed in the bosses of
the driving wheels, or 'inside' (as in Stephenson's *Planet*),
the crankpins being parts of a 'crank axle' which was an expensive component of a locomotive. The centre-lines of inside
cylinders were close together and so the effect of the reciprocating parts in making the engine sway laterally when running
was much less than in an outside-cylinder engine. This was
important in a short engine (and some had only four wheels)
but less so in a ten-wheeler.

As inside cylinders might be between the leading coupled
wheels they permitted use of the 0-6-0 wheel arrangement,
whereas outside cylinders would have to be ahead of the
leading wheels and the resulting overhang led to 'swaying'
and 'porpoising' at any considerable speed.

Inside cylinders were favoured in British practice during
most of the nineteenth century but, at the end of it, the
fundamental superiority of the outside-cylinder scheme was
becoming more attractive to those designers who were con-
templating much larger engines than the current British
average.

Wheels other than driving wheels and coupled wheels were
called 'carrying wheels' and their axles were often allowed
lateral movement in relation to the frame. Such lateral
movement was usually restrained by springs, or by the
horizontal effect of transmitting weight to the axleboxes
through links inclined to the vertical or through inclined
slides. When such an axle was leading, it gently nudged the
locomotive in the direction of every curve just before the
main bulk of the engine had reached it. A single axle of this
type might have hornblocks in a frame called a 'pony-truck'.
The larger frame required to accommodate two such axles
was called a 'bogie'. It was regarded as highly desirable to
provide either a leading bogie or a leading pony-truck for
any locomotive required for regular fast running. Without
such provision there was heavy wear of the flanges of the
leading wheels and of the sides of the rail-heads.

The origin of the power of a steam locomotive was the fire carried on the grate (11) in the bottom of the firebox which was a double-walled downward extension of the boiler. It contained a brick arch (12) kept at bright yellow heat by the hot gases that passed round it on their way to the tubes. Water in the double walls got the full benefit of the intense heat of the fire and most of the steam was produced in those walls and at the top surface (13) (the 'crown-sheet') of the firebox. From the upper part of the front wall of the inner firebox, firetubes (15) about 2 ins in diameter and flues (16) about $5\frac{1}{2}$ ins in diameter extended to the front tubeplate (18) and conveyed hot gases from the firebox to the smoke-box (23) whence they were blown out into the air by exhaust steam shooting upwards in a jet from the blast-pipe (24). All round the tubes and between the inner and outer walls of the firebox was a violent mixture of boiling water and bubbles of steam generated by heat from the white-hot fire and flame in the firebox and the not-quite-so-hot gases in the tubes. In British practice, the inner firebox was made of copper; the rest of the boiler was of steel.

It was essential that the water level be kept above the crown-sheet of the firebox and it was the fireman's prime duty to be sure about this. A crown-sheet over a hot fire, and not protected by water, would be so softened by heat in a minute or so that the pressure of steam would bulge it downwards between the heads of the vertical stays, and then force it clear of them and fracture it with explosive outbursts of steam and water. Last-minute warning of such an accident should be given by the blowing of steam into the firebox through holes made by the melting of fusible plugs fitted in the crown-sheet for this purpose but this was not to be relied on, as was shown by a fatal accident of this kind at Lamington in March 1948. The blowing of steam through the holes left by melted-out plugs in the firebox of an LMS 'Pacific' was heard by at least four locomotive men who knew that something was wrong but nevertheless failed to realize what had happened or that they were in extreme peril.

One of the spring-loaded 'safety valves' (14) was adjusted to 'blow-off' steam when the pressure in the boiler reached the designed 'working pressure'; the second safety valve was usually set for a slightly higher pressure.

Steam passed through the regulator valve (17) at the highest point in the boiler and then through pipes (19) (called superheater elements) about $1\frac{1}{4}$ ins in diameter in the flues. Here the steam was made much hotter and was said to be 'superheated'.

From the superheater, steam passed to one or other of the steam chests (25) containing a valve (26) whose to-and-fro movements in unison with rotation of the wheels allowed steam to enter and to leave the ends of the cylinder (27) at such times as to permit it to do useful work in pushing the piston backwards and forwards in the cylinder.

Each valve was worked by a mechanism called the 'valve gear', by which the driver could cause the steam supply to each end of each cylinder to be cut off when the piston had covered anything from about 5 to 75 per cent of its stroke. To produce the latest cut-off, the valve-travel was given its maximum value; this condition was wasteful of steam but it had to be employed to be sure of starting from rest with a heavy train. As speed rose, the cut-off might be brought earlier, with more efficient use of steam, until it was about 25 per cent of the piston stroke. Earlier cut-offs than this effected no further saving, and below about 15 per cent the steam was again being wastefully used.

To give the valves maximum travel for starting in the forward direction, the driver set the reversing gear in 'full forward gear'. To reduce the travel and make the cut-off early, he set the reversing gear nearer to 'mid-gear' where the cut-off was about 5 per cent; further movement of the reversing gear gave the valves movements appropriate for backward motion of the locomotive. In that condition the reversing gear was in 'backward gear' with the same range of cut-off (about 5 to 75 per cent) as for forward gear. The types of valve gear most commonly used in Britain are shown on p 12.

The maximum opening of the ports to admit steam to the cylinders was very severely reduced as cut-off was brought earlier. Most flat valves and many of the earlier piston valves were too small to permit the maximum power of the engine to be developed on the cut-offs (about 25 per cent) that were necessary for the most economical use of steam.

Flow of steam to the steam chests was controlled by a valve called the 'regulator' (17). A full-open regulator with 20 per cent cut-off could produce the same power output as a partly open regulator with 30 per cent. The persistence for a century of two schools of thought about the relative merits of these methods of working an engine is, in itself, evidence that, in general, there was little to choose between them. Examination of the subject by the methods of elementary physics leads to the same conclusion (Bib. 1).

Except when held up by steam pressure in the superheater-header (20), the 'anti-vacuum valve' (21) was open to admit a flow of air through the superheater and cylinders and out through the chimney, so long as the engine was running; otherwise hot smokebox gas could be drawn into the cylinders where it could carbonize the lubricating oil. In lesser degree this happened when 'drifting' with air drawn through the superheater. For this reason the regulator ought never to have been quite closed when an engine was running, but only on the Great Western (in Great Britain) could engine drivers be persuaded to accept this.

Except for the superheater, and for the fact that flat valves rather than piston valves were common in the nineteenth century, there was nothing in any of this essentially different from what happened in Stephenson's *Planet*. Developments were in size in order to obtain more power, in ability to stand up to higher speeds, and in improved resistance of components to wear.

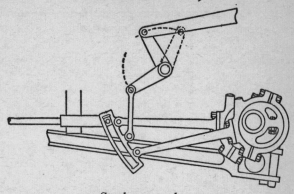

2. Stephenson valve gear

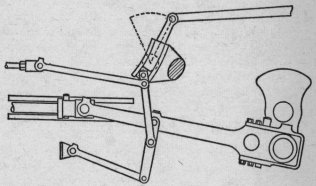

3. Joy valve gear

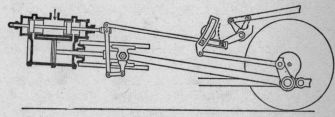

4. Walschaerts valve gear

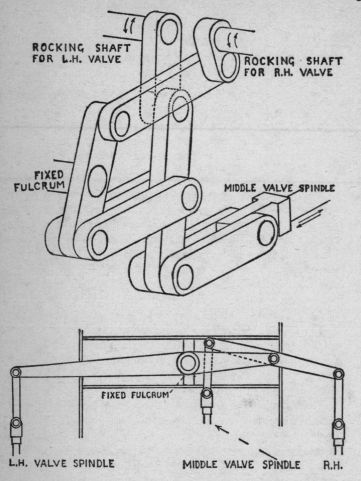

ROCKING SHAFT
FOR L.H. VALVE

ROCKING SHAFT
FOR R.H. VALVE

FIXED
FULCRUM

MIDDLE VALVE SPINDLE

FIXED FULCRUM

L.H. VALVE SPINDLE

MIDDLE VALVE SPINDLE

R.H.

5. Conjugated valve gear for third valve
Upper – as used by Gresley in GN3/2-8-0 No 461 R104
Lower – Plan view of Holcroft arrangement as used in all
other Gresley three-cylinder locomotives with piston valves

THE DOMINANT SIX-WHEELER

The minimum practicable number of wheels for a locomotive is four and this was restrictive because:

(*a*) the total weight had to be limited to about 40 tons as an absolute maximum;

(*b*) if the one advantage of the wheel arrangement (short-ness of wheelbase) were utilized, the overhangs to take cylinders at the front and firebox at the back imposed a low speed limit on the locomotive.

A move to six wheels avoided these restrictions as the firebox could be placed between the second and third axles whilst the other inter-axle space accommodated the mechanism associated with inside cylinders. The addition of two pairs of coupling rods produced the 0-6-0 as the simplest wheel arrangement that enabled all the engine's weight to grip the rails and that admitted of reasonably high speed.

Locomotives of this wheel arrangement formed 46 per cent of the total British railway stock in 1913, 43 per cent in 1922 and 37 per cent in 1947. No other wheel arrangement showed more than half these figures. The numbers of British locomotives, tender and tank, of different wheel arrangements are shown in Fig 6, which demonstrates graphically where lay the weight of locomotive power in Great Britain.

Rational examination of the development of the steam locomotive from 1900 to 1960 might therefore be concentrated on the 0-6-0 because so much money was locked up in it. If this suggestion were to be accepted this account would be short, because the 0-6-0 hardly 'developed' at all, except in size, for a century. There was no need for refinements or sophisticated attachments to it, few of its duties were technically exacting, and elementally simple design and construction sufficed. It was used as a tank engine or a tender engine and in 1900 each group included single-frame engines and double-

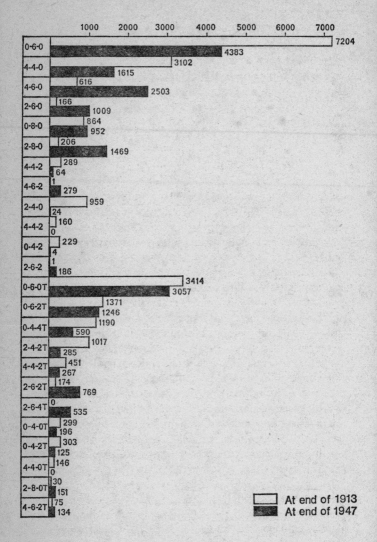

	1000	2000	3000	4000	5000	6000	7000	
0-6-0								7204
				4383				
4-4-0			3102					
	1615							
4-6-0	616							
			2503					
2-6-0	166							
	1009							
0-8-0	864							
	952							
2-8-0	206							
	1469							
4-4-2	289							
	64							
4-6-2	1							
	279							
2-4-0	959							
	24							
4-4-2	160							
	0							
0-4-2	229							
	4							
2-6-2	1							
	186							
0-6-0T			3414					
			3057					
0-6-2T	1371							
	1246							
0-4-4T	1190							
	590							
2-4-2T	1017							
	285							
4-4-2T	451							
	267							
2-6-2T	174							
	769							
2-6-4T	0							
	535							
0-4-0T	299							
	196							
0-4-2T	303							
	125							
4-4-0T	146							
	0							
2-8-0T	30							
	151							
4-6-2T	75							
	134							

At end of 1913
At end of 1947

6. Numbers of locomotives in 1913 and 1947

frame engines. Some had commodious cabs but most did not, and some had none at all.

As almost every railway had 0-6-0s it is not practicable to mention every class nor would there be much object in doing so, as they were all pretty much alike in essentials, but some had points that merit mention. For example, the North Western DX 0-6-0s had grown to a class of 943 by 1874.

The same company's 0-6-0 'coal engines' of which there were 500 by 1892 were probably the simplest six-wheel locomotives ever built and indeed some critics might call them crude. The first of the same company's 'Cauliflower' 0-6-0s (310 in all) was the first locomotive to have Joy valve gear.

The Midland Railway never built anything but 0-6-0s for goods traffic and, by 1923, had over 1,600 of them. The LMS subsequently built several hundred 0-6-0s of the largest Midland design (R2).

All four railway groups had large numbers of 0-6-0 tank engines, the Great Western as many as 1,300 including one class (R135) of 863. By contrast, Great Western 0-6-0 tank engines at work between about 1880 and 1928 exhibited a fantastically large number of variations in detail (Bib. 2).

A new design (R136) of 0-6-0 pannier-tank engine was introduced by this group in 1947 and examples of it were being built as late as 1956. But the new feature in it was merely the combination of pannier tanks (introduced in 1898) with mechanism designed at least as far back as 1897 and a taper boiler dating from 1925. This is perhaps an exceptional example but it does emphasize that for some duties nineteenth-century design methods were as good as any developed later.

Basic design procedure for a 0-6-0 was very simple. First you thought of a wheelbase figure; 15 ft was about right. Then you ascertained from the civil engineer what was the maximum weight he would allow on six wheels so spaced when running on the lightest track in the territory that the engine was to cover. Dividing that by four gave an appropriate nominal tractive effort. Assuming 5 ft for the wheel diameter, 26 ins for the piston stroke and about 180 psi for the boiler pressure one soon found what cylinder diameter was appropriate. If it was less than 18 ins, flat valves could be accommodated between the cylinders and Stephenson valve gear could work the valves.

If cylinders larger than 18 ins were required or if superheated steam were thought useful, then valves would be placed above the cylinders and worked by Stephenson gear through rocking shafts, or by Walschaerts gear if that happened to be in favour at the time, or even by Joy gear.

Whether a reasonably commodious cab were to be provided was a matter of non-technical policy. For running tender first a weatherboard with windows was very acceptable indeed to enginemen but remarkably few British tenders were so provided. The last new design of British 0-6-0, the Southern Q1 (R8) by Bulleid, was well arranged in this respect, and he demonstrated that the intention was that these engines should go fast backwards as well as forwards by having one driven tender-first at 75 mph while he sat on the leading end of it.

On most of the older 0-6-0 tender engines the cab was little more than a weatherboard and even those that looked better than that could be far from ideal. Of the LMS standard 0-6-0s, for example, it was said that in wet weather water came through the roof while ash was blown up towards it through the gaps between the boiler and the footplate. The real virtue of a cab was to keep the weather off the men when the engine was standing, for that was how many 0-6-0s spent a great deal of their time; only the side-window cabs on the North Eastern, Great Eastern, and North British were satisfactory in this respect.

Although the sheer solid worth of the 0-6-0 in all periods is beyond question, its most striking regular work was accomplished in the nineteenth century. For example, as far

back as 1880, Midland o-6-os ran goods trains through the
night from Bradford to London via Leeds (over 200 miles)
at an overall average of 35 mph. At the beginning of the
twentieth century the North Western was so short of engines
for its faster passenger trains that it regularly relied on its
o-6-os to help out.

In 1900 most o-6-os had grate areas less than 20 sq ft but
larger designs were developed later on many railways; the
North Western and the Great Western were exceptions.

Two British classes of o-6-o quite widely separated in
time, the GE 1270 (R6) and the Southern Q1 (R8), had
grate areas of about 27 sq ft and this indicated boiler power
well up to the express passenger train level. The boiler of
the GE o-6-o was, in fact, identical with that of the GE
4-6-os (R34).

It is known that in emergencies o-6-os could run fast
passenger trains quite well, but could they have done it
regularly with complete satisfaction? There are two main
doubts. Firstly, the regular running of a long rigid wheelbase
at speed with no 'pathfinding' wheels in front suggests
severe flange wear on the leading wheels and lateral stress
on the track. Secondly, large, hard-worked o-6-os tended to
suffer overheated axleboxes on the driving axle; in some
angular positions of the cranks the horizontal force on a
'driving' axlebox was considerably greater than the piston-
load. This difficulty could be diminished, in the design
stages, by setting each driving wheel on the axle in the way
that brought the crankpin as close as possible to the adjacent
pin in the crank axle. This placed two heavy revolving
masses on the same side of the axle and it meant increasing
the balance weight in the adjacent wheel. (The crank setting
of the 200-strong 5600 class (R142) of o-6-2T on the Great
Western was changed after service showed axlebox performance to be poor with the original setting.)

Flange wear of the leading wheels could be reduced by
giving the leading axle some axial freedom, under spring

control and inserting vertical hinges in the leading coupling rods.

Design in this way might well have given the 0-6-0 an even wider range of useful duties than it actually had, but nevertheless it is likely that the advantages of avoiding the use of inside cylinders would have caused its eventual abandonment in favour of the 2-6-0. The LMS had adopted this as a policy a few years before nationalization and it was continued by British Railways.

The 0-6-0 could do any railway haulage job at a pinch, but what was its commonest duty? Probably that of running the 'pick-up goods', which was a train of loaded goods vehicles destined for the various stations on a particular length of line. On arrival at each station, the job of the engine would be to take out of the train the vehicles for that station, and to insert, in the right places in the train, vehicles to be taken away from the station. In many cases this would require the whole train to be placed in a siding, so as to leave the running line free while the shunting went on, for it often required more movements and time than a bald statement of its purposes may suggest.

Long-distance haulage of a complete goods train was not so simple as for a passenger train. Any goods train would normally be held several times in sidings or loops to give precedence to passenger trains and, when traffic was heavy, the standing time of a goods train might well exceed its running time. Because of the small brake power on a long train of vehicles not fitted with vacuum brakes or air brakes, the maximum safe speed was not high and so, on an undulating road, the engine would simply be holding the train back for about half the mileage. It would have to pull hard on the up-gradients but at such low speed that the power output was not great. Contrary to what might be suggested by the noisy exhaust of a 'slogging' goods engine, the job was not usually so arduous as that of running the principal passenger trains.

At summer weekends 0-6-0s were quite usually provided for excursion trains and in this service they might run outside their owning company's territory and make longer journeys than their sister passenger train engines normally did. On their own ground and in gay hands, many 0-6-0s could do a mile a minute.

In 1923, Mr C. J. Allen noted a C class 0-6-0 No 581 of the SE to take a gross load of 265 tons in an emergency over the 37·6 miles from Newington, through Rochester, up Sole Street bank, and on to Herne Hill in half a minute less than the 58 minutes allowed, touching 64 mph near Farningham Road (Bib. 3).

In 1963, Midland 4F 0-6-0 No 44386 in an emergency took the 'Waverley' express (about 300 tons) from Appleby to Carlisle 30¾ miles in 34½ minutes start-to-stop with a top speed of 80 mph near New Biggin (Bib. 4).

A North Western 'Cauliflower', well over forty years of age, was observed to reach a maximum of 74 mph in running a passenger train down from Penrith to Carlisle (Bib. 36).

Such spurts were, however, exceptional for 0-6-0s. For most of them life was placid, unexciting, and perhaps stolid. Rather than flashing across the landscape, they tended to be part of it. One Midland 0-6-0, for example, worked from Peterborough shed for over fifty years without a break, apart from periodic visits to Derby works for general repairs.

The duties of 0-6-0 tank engines were mostly in shunting all day in stations, goods yards, and marshalling sidings, and in running trips over short distances. A tender enabled a locomotive to do a full day's work without needing to take on more coal and to do more work between successive calls at water-cranes than could a tank engine, but otherwise the latter was more convenient, especially for shunting. These menial 'odd jobs' formed a much higher proportion of railway work than the man-in-the-street – or even the railway enthusiast – could readily imagine and this is demonstrated by the fact that 0-6-0 tank engines were more than twice as numerous as tank engines of any other wheel arrangement.

The greatest popular interest was always in the latest design of large express train engine and there was plenty of detail development in that field after 1900. Much of this book is therefore devoted to it, but the reader should not forget that the running of the fast passenger trains was only a small fraction of the total locomotive work of any railway. It was popularly interesting, technically interesting, and technically the most difficult part of the work of the motive-power department, but financially it was the least rewarding. Railway officers responsible for goods traffic were resentful of the preference given to passenger trains, and after a lecture on the subject of the LNE streamlined trains (1935–9) one high-ranking railway official referred to them as 'Chief Mechanical Engineer's toys'. The 0-6-0s earned the money.

THE BRITISH 4-4-0

By the year 1900 the 4-4-0 was well established as a wheel arrangement for locomotives for fast passenger trains in Great Britain. There were signs that it might not meet all future requirements in this field; on some railways, however, it actually did so until the grouping of 1923. The 2/4-4-0, ie, the 4-4-0 with no inside cylinders, was much less numerous than the inside cylinder 4-4-0, and the few examples of it still to be built, the GW 'Counties' (R25), were disliked for the rough riding that was only to be expected in an engine with parts reciprocating on centre lines separated by a distance as great as 75 per cent of the rigid wheelbase. But the 'Counties' were not typical British 4-4-0s and they were not even typical Great Western 4-4-0s.

The 4-4-0 was the natural development of the 2-4-0 when demand for greater power would have caused it to be too heavy. The cylinders of a 2-4-0, as those of a 2-2-2 or 0-6-0, were normally placed ahead of the leading axle and the consequent overhang was not ideal for fast running. This did not prohibit high speed on occasion and LNW 2-4-0 *Hardwicke* probably well exceeded ninety between Shap and Carlisle before daybreak on August 23rd, 1895, but the swaying of 2-4-0s and 2-2-2s was not comforting to man, engine, or track. Indeed Great Western 2-2-2 *Wigmore Castle* wiggled herself off the road in Box Tunnel and in consequence she and her sisters were rebuilt as 4-2-2s.

Back in the 1830s the Americans had found a four-wheel bogie to be an excellent means of guiding a locomotive at speed over indifferent track and so the obvious way of avoiding the risks of a heavy 2-4-0 was to build a 4-4-0 instead. It was the simplest way of securing power and speed with safety and the typical British 4-4-0 was a machine of elemental simplicity. The firebox extended deeply downwards between the coupled axles. There was a generous gap between the leading coupled wheels and the trailing bogie wheels and so access to the mechanism between the frame-plates was as good as it could be.

Apart from the North Western examples and a few others, British 4-4-0s had Stephenson valve gear. For cylinder diameters less than about 18 ins, flat valves were used between the cylinders but bigger cylinders prohibited this. One way out was to use Stephenson gear, with or without offsetting arms, to work valves beneath the cylinders and immediately above the bogie, with the plane of the port-faces markedly inclined to the axes of the cylinders. An advantage claimed for this scheme was that the valves fell away from the valve-faces when steam was shut off and this reduced wear. This was quite unconvincing, firstly because, even where the valves were above the cylinders, the pressure on the faces was negligible when steam was shut off, and secondly because normal service did not allow locomotives to cover much of their mileage without steam. The scheme was objectionable in many ways but nevertheless it had a vogue and some notable 4-4-0s incorporated it.

Later on flat valves or piston valves above the cylinders became the normal arrangement with rocking shafts to convey the appropriate motions to the valves from Stephenson valve gear. On the North Western, the 4-4-0s had Joy valve gear which is ideally laid out to operate valves above the cylinders. To give the appropriate motion to piston valves with inside admission, rocking levers were used and, even after it had been realized that they could be avoided by a simple rearrangement of Joy valve gear, they were retained on the 4-4-0s.

In some of the earlier 4-4-0s, with firebox between the axles, the natural centre of gravity was a long way ahead of the rear axle, so the rear end was deliberately ballasted with a thick cast-iron footplate to increase the adhesion weight. In later, larger designs of 4-4-0, the firegrate was inclined so as to lie above the rear axle and to extend behind it, and there was no need for ballast. To obtain adequate firebox volume, and to accommodate fatter boiler barrels, the centre-line of the boiler had to be set higher. Designers tended to be fearful of this at first, but the need for greater power left no alternative and experience did not reveal any special danger in highly pitched boilers.

Successively larger 4-4-0s were developed without difficulty and the type came to be as much a conventional standard for principal passenger trains as the 0-6-0 was for goods trains. On the Midland Railway, in particular, that was precisely the pattern. As late as 1931, long after that railway had been absorbed into the LMS, one might traverse its route from Leeds through Derby and Birmingham to Bristol and see nothing but 4-4-0s and 0-6-0s. The Midland avoided need for larger locomotives by its policies of:

(*a*) running numerous trains instead of long ones; and
(*b*) providing engines to 'double-head' any train that appeared to be even a ton heavier than a very modest limit prescribed for it.

The Midland's young and lusty rival, the Great Central,

started its London main-line passenger train services with
4-4-0s in 1900 and was running its most distinguished trains
with 4-4-0s when it was absorbed into the LNE in 1923 but
it also used a variety of ten-wheelers.

In 1900 the Great Eastern produced the *Claud Hamilton*,
the first of a class of 4-4-0, eventually totalling over a hundred,
that handled its heaviest and fastest passenger trains exclusively till 4-6-0s came on to the scene in 1911. The
'Claud Hamiltons' distinguished themselves particularly in
hauling the 'Norfolk Coast' express non-stop over 130 miles
between Liverpool Street and North Walsham in a scheduled
time of 159 minutes, with a load that was sometimes as
large as 400 tons. This was not quite so remarkable as the
quoted figures may suggest because this job was a specially
starry 'star turn'. Engines allotted to it were specially selected,
kept in specially good order, supplied with specially selected
coal, and handled by three specially selected pairs of men.
With all these advantages, performance even 50 per cent
better than average was only a normal expectation.

By 1905 the latest 4-4-0s on various railways were all
generally similar in essence although showing marked
superficial differences, for example in colour. The observer
would notice rather florid beauty in the 4-4-0s at Liverpool
Street. Brass-capped chimney, brass number-plates with
crimson background and brass-rimmed splashers imposed on
a display of dark-blue paint, all clean and gleaming, would
be sure to impress him.

Coming westwards to St Pancras he would discover
Midland 4-4-0s similar in size to the 'Claud Hamiltons' but
painted in maroon (a rich dignified red) and accompanied by
tenders displaying their engines' numbers in 18-in figures.
He might notice that the coaches were coloured like the
engines. At St Pancras he could see the Midland compound
4-4-0s (R26) but not the corresponding inside-cylinder
simples (R13) as these normally worked only between Leeds
and Carlisle. These engines had the Stévart modification of

Walschaerts valve gear with some feature that was patented by Deeley. With properly dimensioned piston valves in steam-tight condition they could have been the most powerful 4-4-0 'flyers' in Great Britain, but normal performance did not fulfil that expectation.

At Euston all the engines, even the latest 4-4-0s, were black. It was a glossy black with linear decoration in grey and fine red. There were brass number-plates with red background and also brass name-plates showing dignified restraint in size and lettering but not much in choice of names. The 'Precursor' 4-4-0s were good, straightforward, honest-to-God 4-4-0s with blast-pipe and chimney designed so that the limit of power was that set by the will or ability of the fireman to handle the coal. All you had to do to get a big train over the miles was to open everything wide and shovel. A fair proportion of the coal might come white-hot out of the chimney but the work did get done.

The superheated version of the 'Precursors' had the same characteristic but with advantages, and the power that was regularly thrashed out of them would not have been believed by later generations had there been no published records to prove it. Typical of what the 'Georges' (R12) could do when late was the running of No 1595 with a 410-ton train over the 148 miles between Willesden and Betley Road in $143\frac{1}{2}$ minutes with speed reductions to about 40 mph at Rugby and Stafford, beating the booking by about 12 minutes. A regrettable legend about this effort was that it was accomplished on 33 lb of coal per mile whereas normal consumption on such duties was over 60 lb per mile.

Not far away in Marylebone Station (said to be London's best site for quiet meditation) the Great Central 4-4-0s were to be seen in dark green with brass-rimmed splashers and elliptical brass number-plates and with a chimney that conferred a solemn dignity on the whole assembly. Thirty years had to elapse, however, before Great Central 'Director' class 4-4-0s (R15) did their dramatic very bests in swooping over the switchbacks to Manchester with loads twice as heavy as those they took when new.

At Paddington would be found 4-4-0s of the same general dimensions as all the others but markedly different in nearly every detail. Engines of the four railways already mentioned differed from each other in chimneys, domes, safety valves, and cabs. The Great Western 4-4-0s showed further differences that were both greater and more numerous. Here even the boilers differed in being tapered. The safety valves were hidden in brass cones and there was no dome at all. Most of the chimneys were copper-capped but there still remained some shapely iron ones that were favoured for a few years. But the biggest difference of all was that the wheels were hardly visible as they lay behind the eye-catchingly riveted frames and springs and the engines moved with flashing fly-cranks and a tinny tut-tut from the air pump. Yes! the Great Western 4-4-0 was a gorgeous oddity in every respect, even in the fact that it was the first British locomotive to reach 100 mph and the only British 4-4-0 ever to do so.

A different shade of green was to be found on the 4-4-0s of the South Western. Many 2/4-4-0s of Adams design were to be seen but Drummond had already produced 4-4-0s reminiscent of those running on the North British Railway, dour and competent but nothing more in spite of the advantages expected from cross water-tubes in the firebox and a 'steam-drier' in the smoke box. It was not till 1912 that Drummond produced the '463' class (R19), a 4-4-0 distinguished by a 27 sq ft sloping grate and Walschaerts gear working piston valves above the cylinders. This could compete with his latest 4/4-6-0s.

On the Brighton line there were several classes of conventionally dimensioned 4-4-0s with chimney, dome, and safety-valve covers in melting curves so smooth as to seem slimy. They were rather uncertainly displacing the Stroudley 0-4-2s of the 'Gladstone' class from top-rank service. Brown paint was supplanting the striking but rather unpractical brownish yellow known as 'Stroudley's improved engine green'. On July 26th, 1903, one of the larger (class B4) 4-4-0s No 70 (R20) took a special train weighing 130 tons over the 50·9 miles from Victoria to Brighton in 48 min 41 sec, a time never beaten with steam nor even approached in normal service. The top speed of 90 mph would have been startling on this route even sixty years later. This run was made partly to assure the shareholders that the Brighton line need not be significantly outrun by a projected London–Brighton monorail with 100-mph trains.

On the SE the conventional 4-4-0 handled most of the main-line passenger trains. Their distinctive feature was a green-based livery with gay lining and some brass-capped chimneys. Locomotive development was limited by weak underline bridges on some routes but, by 1914, the L class 4-4-0 had appeared and showed external resemblances to both Midland and Great Central locomotives of that wheel arrangement. Ten members of this class were exceptional in British locomotive history in that they were built on the continent of Europe. They were received just before the start of World War I from Borsig of Berlin.

But the really impressive SE 4-4-0s were those produced by Maunsell's rebuilding in 1919 of Wainwright D1 and E1 4-4-0s with new cylinders, right-size piston valves, and a Belpaire boiler with nicely sloped grate (R21). Nearly 50 per cent had been added to the power at speed at the cost of less than half a ton extra weight, but the SE could no longer afford the brass and paint that coloured the Wainwright engines.

The North Eastern had 4-4-0s in considerable numbers and variety, but the group that won for itself the highest reputation was class R (LNE class D20) introduced in 1899. As in earlier North Eastern 4-4-0s the top halves of the two coupled wheels on each side were encased in a wide 'double splasher' that also contained the steam-worked Westinghouse donkey-pump with its head and valve box peeping out of the top.

With piston valves (below the cylinders) and 6 ft 10 in wheels these were free-running engines and round about 1913 they were taking the 'fastest train in the British Empire', the 1.9 PM Darlington to York, over the 44 miles in 43 minutes or less. With loads less than 200 tons the R class 4-4-0s found little difficulty and, on one occasion, No 1672 made the trip inside 40 minutes.

In 1908 that North Eastern introduced the R1 class (R16), which may be described as the biggest British inside-cylinder 4-4-0. It had a special distinction in that each driving axle carried 21 tons whereas the usual British limit in 1908 was 20 tons. With a grate area of 27 sq ft and a 5 ft 6 in boiler the R1 class could be expected to be a superlative 4-4-0 but, in actual fact, even when superheated, its period of service with top-rank North Eastern express trains was short. Its coal consumption was unofficially reported to be high and this may well have been due to leakage past the 10-in outside-admission piston valves. The exhaust sound of an R1 starting from rest suggested 'lost motion' in the valve gear.

On the Lancashire & Yorkshire Railway 4-4-0s were not numerous and none were built after 1900 but one group had coupled wheels 7 ft 3 ins in diameter and a few of these were rebuilt (R17) with superheater and large piston valves worked by Walschaerts gear, but alas! the main elements of the original engine were not strong enough to stand up to the exuberance of the hotted-up rebuild and so maintenance was costly.

On the Caledonian Railway most of the main-line passenger trains were run by 4-4-0s of several classes that were enlarged variants of the 'Dunalastair' of 1896. The 'Dunalastair II' class introduced in 1897 was unique in British practice in being lighter than its fully loaded eight-wheel tender. A few 4-6-0s were used on some of the harder jobs but they never really displaced the 4-4-0s, of which a superheated version was produced by Pickersgill as late as 1916.

The position was similar on the North British Railway where 4-4-0s far outnumbered the 'Atlantics' that normally handled the most important passenger trains. On the Glasgow & South Western there were about twenty 2/4-6-0s but many more 4-4-0s. The Highland Railway favoured the 2/4-4-0 rather than the 4-4-0. The Great North of Scotland Railway used 4-4-0s for both passenger trains and goods trains and had no tender engines of any other wheel arrangement.

On every main line there were examples of the ordinary British 4-4-0, weighing about 50 tons, having about 20 sq ft of grate area with cylinders about 19 ins in diameter and coupled wheels about 7 ft high. All railways relied on them for haulage jobs that were generally similar although not identical, and the 4-4-0s could do what was wanted. When equipped with superheater and piston valves, 4-4-0s became better than ever and on some lines not even the later and larger 4-6-0s could beat them.

Nevertheless, very few inside-cylinder 4-4-0s were built for British railways after World War I. The Great Western introduced in 1936 some saucy little double-frame 4-4-0s entirely in the Victorian style of William Dean but they were not really new engines. The design was the result of fitting 'Bulldog' undercarriages with 'Duke' boilers to produce an engine not too heavy for service on the Cambrian section of the Great Western Railway. By some students of the locomotive the 'Earls' were derided as unimaginative throwbacks, while others were delighted with their promise of prolongation of a fascinating phase in Great Western history, but there was nothing in the whole world-railway scene to surpass the stirring beauty of a sparkling 'Earl' doing 'seventy' along the scenic valley of the Severn between Newtown and Welshpool.

In 1927 Gresley produced the first of the 3/4-4-0s (R27) known as LNE class D49, with his conjugated valve gear mounted behind the steam chests and with the drive from

the pistons on to the leading coupled wheels and axle.
Gresley is said to have disliked a crank in the leading coupled
axle because there it would be subjected to bending moment
produced by flange force on either wheel. (This, if true,
suggests that as was common British practice for a long
time, the side-control forces on the bogie were not so strong
as they might usefully have been.) There was, however, no
choice in a 3/4-4-0.

Location of the conjugated gear behind the steam chests
left easier access for withdrawal of the valves for periodic
examination. There was plenty of room for a man to get to
the inside mechanism by passing between a bogie wheel and
the next coupled wheel without needing a pit between the
rails.

A later version of the D49s had poppet valves worked by
cams in boxes above the steam chests. In some of these the
camshafts were given a semi-rotary motion by Walschaerts
gear and Gresley gear. In others, the camshafts were given a
common continuous rotation by wormgears, carried in a box
suspended on an arm extending radially inwards from the
right-hand driving crankpin. A longitudinal shaft connected
the gearbox to the cambox. In these engines it was almost
as easy to get to the driving mechanism inside the frame as to
that outside it.

A special version of the 4-4-0 was the three-cylinder
compound (R26) introduced on the Midland in 1902. With
sundry modifications it became the 'ace' locomotive of that
company and its sponsors had such control in the LMS,
that that group added 195 compounds to the Midland's 45
so that they were eventually both the most numerous
British compound engines and the most numerous British
4-4-0s of any description. The Midland policy of never
goading engines prevented the compounds from showing
all they could do, but in the more realistic atmosphere of the
one-time rival routes between Carlisle and Glasgow there
was no such restraint. There the compounds were thrashed

whether they liked it or not and the results convinced some delighted amateurs that Scottish drivers had a skill not to be found elsewhere.

But it seemed that if three cylinders were to be used they were wasted in a compound, as the Southern 'School' three-cylinder 4-4-0 (R28), introduced in 1930, left all other British 4-4-0s well behind. A locomotive with grate area of $28\frac{1}{2}$ sq ft, nominal tractive effort of 26,000 lb, and best speed range of 57–79 mph, if properly designed, built, and operated could be expected to rival the Great Western 'Star' class 4/4-6-0 (R65) which had dominated British locomotive performance at least from 1908 to 1923. The 'Schools' did this, surpassing all other 4-4-0s and many 4-6-0s. Dimensionally they justified the playful name 'three-quarter Nelson' but in service they were nearer to a 'full Nelson' (R75) except in starting and other hard pulling, where their smaller adhesion weight was an unavoidable restriction.

In the 'Schools' the firemen had the uniformly sloping grate that they were used to feeding. It was 25 per cent bigger than that of the North Western 'George' but no harder to fire, the nominal tractive effort was high enough to make economic use of all the steam that the thrashed boiler could produce and so it was no surprise that when put to it, a 'School' might deliver 25 per cent more power than a 'George'.

It must be emphasized that here we have touched on a few special points of interest about particular classes of 4-4-0 and about some of their performances. Most of their work could claim no outstanding distinction but its value may be judged from the fact that, in 1913, there were in Britain over 3,000 4-4-0s constituting 46 per cent of all tender locomotives other than 0-6-0s, and 25 per cent of all locomotives other than 0-6-0s and 0-6-0Ts.

TEN-WHEELERS

For most of the life of the steam locomotive, development had
to be in the direction of more power, which meant bigger
engines. But the strength of rails and bridges had not
increased proportionately to the demands for more power,
and larger locomotives were possible only by increasing the
number of axles and also the total wheelbase so that the
greater weight was spread over a greater length of track.
In the nineteenth century, six-wheel engines predominated
but eight-wheelers were becoming common towards the
end and, by 1900, ten-wheelers had also appeared. One
question was whether the ten-wheeled express passenger
train engine should be four-coupled or six-coupled, ie,
4-4-2 ('Atlantic') or 4-6-0. Many of the lighter trains running
over easily graded lines were being economically handled
by engines each with a single pair of driving wheels. Coupling
together the wheels of a high-speed engine was thought to
introduce a great deal of extra friction and, whilst four-
coupling was tolerated, six-coupling was feared, despite its
advantage in permitting the adhesion weight (on the driving
and coupled wheels) to be over 50 tons and thus affording
enough rail-grip to start (say) a 400 ton train on a 1 in 50
gradient.

An obvious source of doubt about longer locomotives was
their behaviour on sharp curves. Lateral flexibility was
clearly valuable or even necessary in those conditions and it
was provided by using bogies or pony-trucks with some lateral
freedom in relation to the main frame. In going on from eight-
wheel engines to a new ten-wheel design, this point was one
that caused designers some concern. It was natural, therefore, to use the 4-4-2 wheel arrangement in preference to the
4-6-0 in the earliest British ten-wheel engines as the provision of side-play in a rear-coupled axle is more complicated
than if it is only a carrying axle.

The first British ten-wheel tender locomotive for passenger train service was the Great Northern 4-4-2 No 990 built in 1898 (and later known as the 'small Atlantic') which was largely an elongation of a Stirling 4-2-2. Outside cylinders were used, the boiler looked long and slender and the engines were never brilliant performers.

The second British ten-wheel design was also a 4-4-2, the Lancashire & Yorkshire, No 1400 (R105). This was a lengthened and heightened version of the standard Lancashire & Yorkshire 4-4-0 with 7 ft 3 in driving wheels. Inside cylinders were used and the driving mechanism and valve gear were interchangeable with those of the 4-4-0s. Few people can now discern anything beautiful about the Lancashire & Yorkshire 'Atlantics' but they did their work well and no other Horwich design bettered it in twenty years. The trailing axle initially had inside axleboxes but these were later replaced by outside boxes which, being in cooling draughts well away from the heat of the ashpan, were less likely to overheat. These Aspinall 'Atlantics' would get up to 90 mph or so (rumours of 100 mph were not well founded) down the moderate slopes of the Lancashire & Yorkshire route between Liverpool and Manchester but the loads were very light and never demanded very high power output. In later years these engines took much heavier trains over the lines from Manchester to Blackpool and to Southport. Their uphill work sadly puzzled those people who accepted the hoary fable that big wheels were bad for hill climbing.

The North Eastern was the first English railway to use large-wheeled 4-6-0s for passenger trains, but later concentrated on 4-4-2s. The Great Northern, associated with the North Eastern as a co-partner in the East Coast route, adopted an enlarged version (R107) of the '990' class 'Atlantic' and never used the 4-6-0. The other partner in the East Coast route, the North British, graduated from 4-4-0 to 4-4-2 in 1906 and never used the 4-6-0.

The large Great Northern 'Atlantics', the North Eastern

'Atlantics', and the Great Western 4-6-0s and 'Atlantics'
introduced to their systems boilers 5 ft 6 ins in diameter and
these appeared so large at the time that it was asserted by
some unimaginative commentators that these engines were
as big as the British loading gauge would permit.

The North Eastern two-cylinder 'Atlantics' were heavy on
coal but otherwise undistinguished. The Great Northern
'Atlantics' were heavy on coal and wiggled their way along
the road in the most dangerous-looking manner possible
without actually wiggling off it. The North British Atlantics
(R111) equalled (and sometimes surpassed) the others in
coal consumption and rode fairly violently.

The bad riding of the Great Northern 'Atlantics' is fully
explained by the absence of side-control for the trailing axle
and by the extremely short rigid wheelbase. (A penny could
be made to touch the flanges of two coupled wheels at once.)
There was nothing to stop the back end of the engine from
swaying from side to side and so it swayed.

The fireman of a Great Northern 'large Atlantic' was partly
reconciled to the swaying by the fact that it kept the fire
nicely spread over the wide grate. If you could only get the
coal through the firehole, the oscillation would do the rest.
Moreover, the tender was also sufficiently jiggled by the
engine to keep the footplate (such as it was) deep in coal.
A suitably shaped piece of steel plate ledged on the tender and
the firehole ring would have formed the simplest mechanical
stoker ever devised.

These early 'Atlantics' did not at first show much improvement on the work of the 4-4-0s that preceded them. The
North Eastern and North British classes were slightly sluggish
but the Great Northern engines had the saving graces of
free steaming and a fair turn of speed. They had the biggest
grate area of the three classes, a blast-pipe nicely constructed
to produce a sharp blast that could really pull air through
the fire, they were easy to fire, and rarely short of steam. The
cylinders and valves were so small in relation to the boiler

that its full output could be absorbed at ordinary running speeds only by working at late cut-off, and the long valve-travel associated with this gave plenty of opening to exhaust through the backs of flat valves. The steam was used fairly wastefully but there was plenty of it and so the engines could run fast in easy conditions. In respect of grate area the 'large Atlantics' were ahead of all other standard types of passenger train engine in Britain for ten years.

In later years, with larger cylinders, piston valves, and big superheaters, and with Gresley 'Pacifics' to set the pace, the Ivatt (Great Northern) 'Atlantics' were hammered along in ruthless style with loads far bigger than they ever took in their first few years. This was practicable because, unless something was wrong, they maintained full boiler pressure however hard they were thrashed provided that the fire was fed as fast as it burned the coal; they were pretty well foolproof. The big loads emphasized the poor starting abilities of these engines (and of most 'Atlantics'), for with carrying wheels fore and aft the weight on the coupled wheels was an uncertain quantity and starting on an upgrade was a correspondingly uncertain operation. An Ivatt 'Atlantic', superheated and in good condition, having run 175 miles from London on time with the 'West Riding Pullman', could occupy three minutes in covering a quarter of a mile between a signal stop and Wakefield Westgate Station. For all that, when over twenty-five years old they did much good work on long non-stop runs, far better, probably, than Ivatt himself could have expected. In one particular 'all-out' effort, made in an emergency that excused the driver for any maltreatment of the engine, No 4404 took a train of 585 tons over the 76½ miles northwards from Barkston to Chaloner Whin Junction on the East Coast main line at an average speed of 61·3 mph. Another engine of the class took 565 tons from Doncaster to Peterborough, 80 miles at 59·2 mph start-to-stop.

A much-emphasized advantage of the 4-4-2 wheel

arrangement over the 4-6-0 was that the firebox might extend laterally over the rear carrying wheels instead of being confined to an overall width of about 4 ft, as was the case when (as usual) it lay within the ordinary plate frame. The wide box minimized the length required for any desired grate area, and minimum length was evidently important in the design of the Ivatt 'Atlantics'. The side view shows a boiler that thoroughly filled the wheelbase and left the unfortunate enginemen with a very short footplate. This was a large engine for 1903 with nevertheless the general impression of grace rather than excessive bulk and the popular acclaim of the type is readily understood. It was always a favourite of enginemen, despite its discomfort, and the design is one of the most notable in the whole history of the steam locomotive.

It was copied faithfully by D. Earle Marsh when he had left Doncaster to take charge of the locomotive department of the London Brighton & South Coast Railway and the eleven Brighton 'Atlantics' were the only British 'Atlantics' besides the large Ivatt ones to have wide fireboxes.

It should be added that, even if the narrow firebox is used, the 4-4-2 wheel arrangement admits a deeper firebox than can be placed over the higher rear axle of the corresponding 4-6-0.

'Atlantics' built by the Great Western showed no advantage over the 4-6-0s to offset the disadvantage of smaller adhesion weight and were, accordingly, converted to 4-6-0s. The Great Central also had 4-4-2s and 4-6-0s of common major dimensions but found no difference great enough to justify a change from either to the other. On that line, however, passenger-train loads never exceeded the reasonable capacity of a four-coupled engine.

The North Eastern two-cylinder 'Atlantics' were large but not proportionately effective. The three-cylinder 4-4-2s (R112) produced by Raven for that railway did far better work.

Nearly all British 'Atlantics' had two outside cylinders and no others. Exceptional classes were the North Eastern class Z with three cylinders and the LY '1400' class with two inside cylinders.

On the other hand, British 4-6-0s appeared in considerable numbers with two inside cylinders, two outside cylinders, three cylinders, or four cylinders. In nearly all cases, the firegrate lay over the rear axle and extended forwards and downwards within the limit imposed by the middle coupled axle. Exceptions (see p 53) were:

(1) the LSW four-cylinder 4-6-0s and the LNW two-cylinder 4-6-0s in which the grate lay horizontally over the middle coupled axle; and

(2) the GE 4-6-0s in which the grate was horizontal behind the middle coupled axle but sloped downwards thence towards the leading coupled axle.

A long horizontal grate was hard to fire and the South Western 4/4-6-0s were doomed to mediocrity by their 10-ft horizontal grates even apart from their other defects. The 8-ft long grates of the North Western 4-6-0s, of which hundreds were built, were not quite so bad in this respect, but they were much harder to fire than were the grates of the 'George' and 'Claughtons'. Moreover, the best work of the 'Princes' (R31) surpassed that of the rather larger GE 4-6-0s (R34) with partly sloping grates.

Because the drive in a 4-6-0 was naturally to cranks on the leading coupled axle, whereas in a 2/4-6-0 it was naturally to the middle coupled axle, the former tended to have a longer wheelbase and some designers were tempted by this to make the firetubes longer than they should have been. One result was that on the CR and GC the advantage of 4-6-0s over 4-4-0s was barely discernible and in the latter case not even positive. On each railway 2/4-6-0s did better than the 4-6-0s, but even then not brilliantly.

The 4-6-0s with short boiler barrels (LNW and GE) performed much more convincingly and considerable numbers of those engines were in main-line service for many years.

A big 4-6-0 applied heavy horizontal loads to the driving axleboxes, and although this could be mitigated by in-line setting of outside and inside crankpins on the leading axle (as was done in the GE engines), outside cylinders driving the middle coupled wheels avoided the difficulty. The point is that connecting-rod thrust on an outside crankpin was opposed by thrusts in the adjacent coupling-rods which thus relieved the axleboxes of a good deal of horizontal load, whereas, with inside cranks as normally set, coupling-rod thrust was added to the axlebox load produced by piston thrust.

Some designers of large-wheeled 4-6-0s showed inadequate appreciation of the need to provide easy access of air to the underside of the firegrate. The original LY 4/4-6-0s and nearly all the varieties of GC 4-6-0s were throttled by inadequate air-passages and accumulation of ash where the bottom of the ashpan lay close to the firebars. There was no trouble of this kind in the Great Western ten-wheelers because the difficulty had been anticipated and the ashpan was therefore given four air inlets and no place where ash could lodge near the firebars (p 53).

Churchward on the Great Western had showed by 1906 what a British 2/4-6-0 could be (R37) and by 1942 even the LNE (firmly wedded for years to wide fireboxes and three cylinders) began to produce such locomotives for general service.

Churchward also developed a 4/4-6-0 (R65) with the same boiler as the 2/4-6-0 and the better balancing of the former led him to use it for the fastest trains, despite its higher cost in building and maintenance. This limited the opportunities for demonstrating the full abilities of the 2/4-6-0 on the hardest Great Western duties, but it did not restrain the Great Western from building hundreds of 2/4-6-0s for more general service.

On the South Western, and particularly between Salisbury

and Exeter, the '736' class (R48) of 2/4-6-0 produced by Urie in 1918 was the best engine for the heaviest passenger train duties on that line till 1925, but it needed Maunsell's modifications that produced the 'King Arthurs' (R55) to show the 2/4-6-0 at its best on the Southern Railway.

With a sloping grate of about 30 sq ft and with no rear carrying wheels to make coupled wheel adhesion uncertain, the 2/4-6-0 was a widely useful locomotive and multiplication to a total of over 800 class 5 2/4-6-0s (R53) on the LMS showed how highly it was esteemed on that system.

Nationalization was only five years ahead when the LNE first took an interest in the 2/4-6-0 but it produced over 400 of the B1 class (R54) similar in size and general form to the LMS class 5 4-6-0, although its parallel boiler barrel and round-topped firebox, 'throttled' by an unnecessarily high running-board, made it look very weak by comparison.

After 1923 the toughest haulage jobs on British main lines were entrusted to locomotives with more than two cylinders and so in that period the best efforts in relation to size were not made by two-cylinder engines. Nevertheless Appendix 3 shows a Great Western 'Saint' (R37) to have been not far behind Great Western 4/4-6-0s in this assessment of power for size and an LMS class 5 2/4-6-0 to have made a comparable effort during an early attempt to find what these engines could do.

The main disadvantage of a 2/4-6-0 pressed hard at speed was the bad knock that resulted from slackness produced by wear of the sliding surfaces of the axlebox in the hornblocks. This was fatiguing for the enginemen and discouraged them from working the engine any harder than was necessary to escape severe criticism from their immediate superiors.

The 4-6-0 wheel arrangement was limited to a grate area of about 35 sq ft on which coal could be burned as fast as a fireman could reasonably be expected to feed it for two or three hours at a stretch. The power output could meet all

British requirements and so there was no need to build anything bigger than 4-6-0s for journeys up to about 200 miles. For longer trips, eg, London to Glasgow or Edinburgh, deterioration of a fire of inferior coal could be serious and this justified grate areas up to 50 sq ft and therefore the adoption of the 4-6-2 wheel arrangement.

It may be suggested that the form that a 'first-line' ten-wheeler might best have taken was that of a rebuilt 'Scot' sufficiently stretched to make the rear of the inside cylinder reasonably accessible by placing the cylinder in line with the others, and with the same nominal tractive effort and optimum speed-ranges as the Gresley A4. Figure C, p 161, shows such a design with wheelbase similar to that of an LMS proposal in 1924 for a 3C/4-6-0, and with boiler pressure reduced to 180 psi, permitting the boiler to be fattened and the firebox lengthened without increase in weight.

Away from the mainstream of development was a ten-wheeler introduced on the LNE in 1936. This was the Gresley class V2 3/2-6-2 (R129) conceived as a compromise between the 3/2-6-0 of class K3 and the 3/4-6-2 of class A3. It was a kind of 'pocket Pacific' capable of high power at high or medium speeds and was sufficiently satisfactory for 184 to be built. Although no one really trusted two-wheel pony-trucks at speed, the V2s sometimes ran at over 90 mph and the only high-speed derailment that got a V2 into the news (Hatfield, July 15th, 1946) had remarkably slight consequences.

CHAPTER TWO

GENERAL DEVELOPMENT

APART FROM increases in size and adoption of different wheel arrangements, worthwhile locomotive development in Great Britain since 1900 may be summarized thus:

1. *Superheating*
This was generally accepted by 1910. Changes after then were only in details, such as the form and fixing of the 'elements'. Dampers to protect the elements when without steam, and pyrometers to indicate the temperature of the steam were tried but rejected as superfluous.

2. *Piston Valves*
Difficulty of lubricating flat valves working in superheated steam demanded the development of piston valves (long recognized as desirable even with 'wet' steam) in a reliable form. This was a more difficult problem than it looked (even Churchward was beaten for a time) and hundreds of locomotives laboured for millions of miles with piston valves that leaked badly between examinations at intervals of 20,000 miles. One solution reached (for example) by the LMS in the 1930s following a twenty-year lead in Germany, was the use of half a dozen of the old Ramsbottom piston rings.

Success depended on using an appropriate grade of cast iron for the piston rings and the steam-chest liners.

3. *Size of Valves*
Adoption of valve dimensions that permitted the attainment of the highest possible cylinder efficiency when developing full power at the highest running speed at which it would

normally be required in service. This demanded longer
valve travel than had been conventional and fear of this
produced spirited opposition to advancement in this field.
No working formula on this subject was published until after
World War II (eg, Bib. 5).

4. *Axleboxes*

Adoption of axleboxes of such design, dimensions, materials,
and construction as to enable them to work, without 'running
hot', for many thousands of miles before requiring attention.

5. *Valve Gear*

Adoption of Walschaerts valve gear for valves over outside
cylinders. Such a gear was easily accessible and, appropriately
designed and made, cost little to keep in order.

6. *Design for Minimum Deterioration*

Modification of design details with the object of increasing
the mileage that a locomotive could run between successive
major repairs. A target was 100,000 miles, but this was never
quite reached regularly by any class of British locomotive.

7. *Economic Repair Work*

Development of systematic procedure in periodic repairs of
locomotives. A major advance in this field was the adoption in
1928 of the 'belt' system for locomotive repairs at Crewe
Works.

SOME COMMENTS ON DESIGN

The satisfactory service of any machine depends primarily on
sound materials, good workmanship in manufacture, and con-
scientious care in maintenance. With all these assured, one
can reasonably direct attention to details of design and can
become so engrossed in them, large and small, as to overlook
the fundamental essentials. They tend to be taken for granted.

Within the sphere of design, the corresponding condition is that apparently small details, often left to the care of junior draughtsmen, can be more important than the major dimensions (ie, dimensions of large components) that were usually published.

For example, the heating surface is a dimension of a locomotive boiler that was always quoted but, in respect of power output, it was far less important than the width of the water-spaces that surrounded the firebox and that separated the firetubes. These last two dimensions could be ascertained from sectional drawings but it was most uncommon for the figures to be included in any published list of dimensions.

Commentators failed for a long time to appreciate the obvious fact that heating surface was not a generator of heat but only a transmitter. It could not transmit any more heat than was presented to it, and a moment's reflection shows that the basic measure of the maximum power of a steam locomotive is the maximum rate at which heat can be generated in its firebox. This may seem obvious enough, but published work makes it clear that many writers (both amateur and professional) had not grasped this simple fact. It was here that a little practical experience could bring enlightenment. No one who had tried to fire a locomotive that was working a bit too hard for him was in any doubt as to the origin of the power.

This was the heart of the enginemen's first problem, that of making the engine 'steam'. A locomotive was said to be 'steaming' when it generated steam as fast as it used it, so that the boiler pressure remained at or near the limit set by the safety valves, without demanding hair-splitting precision in every detail of the fireman's work. Whether an engine 'steamed' or not on any particular day depended partly on certain details in design, partly on the amount of dirt on its heating surfaces and in its firetubes, partly on the quality of coal it was burning, partly on the skill and endurance of the fireman, and not at all on the size of the cylinders.

Apart from loss by leakage, all the steam produced by the boiler came out of the blast-pipe and went up the chimney, dragging products of combustion with it. If the cross-sectional area of the blast-nozzle were reduced, without change in the evaporation rate, the steam came faster out of the nozzle and so was able to induce air-flow through the fire at a higher rate than before.

To improve the steaming of an engine it was common (but unofficial) practice to fix a stout wire or a strip of steel across the top of the blast-nozzle in order to reduce its effective area. This was a quick, simple 'on the spot' remedy for emergency use. The official counterpart, applied to any class of engine that normally steamed badly, was to replace the blast-pipe cap by a smaller one and (for real refinement) also to reduce the internal diameter of the chimney itself. Because these changes were inexpensive (in relation to the whole cost of the locomotive) the designer did not need to lose much sleep over the task of settling the dimensions of these particular components when developing the design. He naturally preferred to get them right first time, but what was 'right' might be difficult to decide. Restricting the blast-nozzle improved the steaming but increased the coal consumption per unit of work done. The increase was smaller than some writers seemed to imagine, but it must be mentioned here in order to explain why no designer would be justified in plumping for a very small blast-nozzle in the first instance. The ideal was the largest nozzle that would enable the engine to steam at full power in conditions somewhat inferior to the normal ones. If average conditions deteriorated over the years, what was originally satisfactory might cease to be so and should be changed. Successful modification of the 'draughting' of Great Western locomotives in the 1950s was not a reason for criticism of the original draughting of 1906.

Design for adequate steaming is mentioned here to emphasize that cylinder volume was not at all critical, despite what commentators sometimes said and what might be falsely deduced from pathetic fiddling with cylinder size in certain unsatisfactory locomotives. Every cylinder was increased in diameter by anything up to an inch by successive reboring during its life. This was normal practice.

The 'nominal tractive effort' of a locomotive was not a measure of its power; it is regrettable that there was a legend (for which Great Western publicity in the 1920s was largely to blame) to the opposite effect. It is depressing to find amateurs believing that one class of engine was superior to another because it had a nominal tractive effort of (say) 28,673 lb as against 27,798 lb in its competitor. Because of inevitable uncertainties in the basic dimensions it is absurd to quote nominal tractive effort to any smaller unit than 1,000 lb and, moreover, variations of twice that amount made no perceptible difference to performance except perhaps when slogging 'all out' at very low speed.

Only after about the year 1940 did it become usual to quote, among published dimensions of a locomotive, the lap of the valves or the cross-sectional area available for passage of products of combustion through the firetubes. This reflects the late realization by some designers of the importance of these dimensions.

Design and materials of axleboxes showed wide differences of practice between different British railways before 1923 and some of them persisted nearly till nationalization in 1948. There should be no hole or groove of any sort in the load-carrying part of the bearing surface of an axlebox, and the white-metal lining should be thin rather than thick if it is not to be badly deformed by the heavy loads set up by repeated piston thrusts. Oil should be fed to the underside of the axle where there is no load on it. This was known (to some people) well back in the nineteenth century, but many pre-grouping designs suggested that it was unknown even in the twentieth century to some designers who could have made good use of it.

Axleboxes between the wheels were well hidden in a steam locomotive and the amateur observer naturally spared no thought for them, but any defect in design or materials of axleboxes could be costly in regular maintenance and might greatly increase the risk of engine failure by a 'hot box'. This was overheating and partial or complete melting of the white metal as a result of failure of the oil supply; not until the 1930s had widespread application of correct design practically eliminated 'hot boxes'.

Friction between axleboxes and hornblocks led to wear that produced slackness of the boxes which then suffered two or more violent impacts during each revolution of the driving wheels. Strong vibration from this cause was extremely unpleasant and fatiguing for the enginemen and tended to shake the locomotive itself into its individual components. So a close watch had to be kept on wear of this kind.

But even locomotives that could easily have been designed in such a way as to save 20 per cent of their actual coal consumption might be quite reasonably efficient in overall cost, because good detail design made their failures rare and their maintenance cheap and easy. Substantial advantages of this kind were obtained by making everything as easily accessible as possible, regardless of appearance, and it is a pity that British practice was so late in thus departing from the Victorian principle of keeping everything (except the enginemen) out of sight.

American practice was always sensible in this respect, but conventional aesthetics prevented British designers from following it until stark economics took the upper hand.

Those whose work it is to assemble machinery and, even more emphatically, those who have to dismantle machinery and to reassemble it after repair have frequent cause to complain that no care seems to be taken in designing machines so as to minimize the labour involved in such operations. Locomotive design is no exception in this respect and a reason for it may be discerned in the following extract from an address given by R. E. L. Maunsell, then chief mechanical engineer of the SE, to the Institution of Locomotive Engineers on January 29th, 1916:

> Taking into consideration therefore the number of different aspects from which a draughtsman must view the work on which he is engaged, and the fact that in 99 cases out of a 100 he has had no footplate or even running-shed experience, it is not surprising to hear sometimes of a new class of engine being somewhat severely criticized by the staff responsible for its running, maintenance and operation, notwithstanding the fact that *when* it is at work it is capable of performing its duty economically and well.

One may be permitted to comment that a railway company that obtained its draughtsmen by promotion of juniors was in a position to make sure that they did get, at some stage, the practical experience in building and repairing locomotives that would make them less likely to produce awkward designs. Even so, it is a fact that conditions sometimes make it impossible to produce a design that is satisfactory in every detail.

EARLY TRENDS

At the end of the nineteenth century, British locomotive practice was entering on the last phase of its development. Six-coupled locomotives were coming along for passenger-train service, and eight-coupled ones for freight; superheating, already in successful use in Germany, was not far away, and tolerably good piston valves had been developed. Within ten years one British railway at least had worked these features into sound designs that were never substantially surpassed, so that by the start of World War I the peak of development had been reached and the only further changes were in size and in cleaning up of details.

The principle of compounding, already badly discredited by what Webb was doing with it on the North Western, was to be decisively rejected by Churchward after trials on the Great Western, but accepted to a limited extent on the Midland where, with no initial competition from any distinguished design of single-expansion locomotive, it was to survive for half a century.

Passenger trains were mostly handled by 2-4-os and 4-4-os, with temporary assistance, on some lines, from o-6-os. Most lines were making considerable use of 'single-driver' locomotives and not only were some of them only a year or two old, but the last new design of 'single-driver' had not yet appeared. Apart from this (Ivatt's 4-2-2 on the Great Northern), however, 'singles' were to be abandoned rather rapidly and only a very few were ever fitted with superheaters.

Boilers had already begun to be too fat to lie between the driving wheels and the high pitch that this made necessary was compelling the use of chimneys markedly shorter than any previously seen in Great Britain. Outside cylinders were coming into fashion after fifty years of British preference for inside ones. Conversely, double-frame locomotives were being rapidly scrapped (except on the Great Western) and so outside axleboxes were becoming less common, except on tenders where they continued to be preferred and on non-driving axles beneath the ashpan.

There was no marked trend in the direction of faster timing of trains but new passenger vehicles were being given more weight per seat and passengers themselves were still becoming more numerous. So every locomotive superintendent was faced with the need to provide more powerful locomotives, and the years from 1900 to 1914 produced much of great interest to both professional and amateur. The pages of *The Locomotive* for this period show new designs of locomotive appearing at a rate never approached since then and barely imaginable in the 1960s.

GOODS ENGINES

Because high speed was neither required nor permissible in British loose-coupled goods trains, the 0-6-0 wheel arrangement sufficed for such service until a need arose to run trains beyond the tractive effort of even the heaviest permissible 0-6-0. The obvious next move was to the 0-8-0 wheel arrangement and that was used by the North Western Railway in considerable numbers before 1900. Soon afterwards eight-coupled goods engines, 0-8-0, 2/0-8-0 and 2/2-8-0 appeared on several British railways and on few of them was there any subsequent need for any larger locomotive for goods service. Eight-coupled goods engines in general lasted for many years, largely because goods engines spent a good deal of time standing still, rarely ran fast, and rarely produced high power in relation to size.

On the Great Western the standard 2/2-8-0 had a boiler and cylinders identical with those of the standard 2/4-6-0s but this ideal condition was not attained on all railways.

Something with a bigger firebox than could be placed on an eight-coupled engine was deemed to be useful in coping with inferior coal and maintenance during World War II; after nationalization some 250 2/2-10-0s were built, over a quarter of the total number of British Railways standard locomotives.

MIXED TRAFFIC ENGINES

Although an 0-6-0 could perform reasonably well in every class of service in emergency, neither the engine nor the track liked it very much when the speed was high. So the 2/2-6-0 was a better 'mixed-traffic' locomotive and several British railways built such engines in considerable numbers. Although the type was not unknown in Britain before 1899, it appeared rather dramatically in that year in the form of imports from America for the Midland, the Great Northern, and the Great Central railways. These engines would have been o-6-os had the American manufacturers been used to that wheel arrangement but they were not, because the early American railway tracks were not good enough to retain a locomotive at speed unless it had a leading truck.

The 2/2-6-o as a mixed-traffic locomotive in a design that persisted, appeared first in the Great Western 4300 class in 1911 and was built in large numbers by that railway, by the Great Northern, and by the LMS. Elaborated to 3/2-6-o it was developed on the Great Northern and multiplied on the LNE.

But mixed-traffic requirements were met on other railways by 2/4-6-os with driving wheels about 6 ft in diameter and the H15 class of 2/4-6-o on the LSW (R47) with Walschaerts valve gear was the pioneer of what came to be accepted as the best form of the mixed-traffic locomotive for British service. After British Railways had built over 250 class 4 and class 5 2/4-6-os there were about 2,000 mixed-traffic 2/4-6-os in Great Britain.

TANK ENGINES

For short journeys, the coal and water required by a steam locomotive could be contained in a bunker and tanks carried on its frame, and no tender was necessary. Such a 'tank engine' could run backwards with no tender to push and this was an advantage where the daily duty included many reversals of the direction of motion.

The majority of tank engines were small, but, after 1900, several railways built fairly large 4-4-2Ts and 2/4-4-2Ts with driving wheels big enough to cope with running at 75 mph. By 1914 two designs of 2/4-6-4T were in service. Before the grouping of 1923, 4-6-4Ts and further 2/4-6-4Ts had been added. In 1924 the LMS built 4/4-6-4Ts each weighing nearly 100 tons (R196). Of these large tank engines the most successful were the Brighton 2/4-6-4Ts (R193) but only after persistent bad riding had persuaded Billinton to provide each engine with a well-tank under the boiler and to cut down the water capacity of the side-tanks almost to zero.

In this form the engines were used for some twenty years on the fastest London–Brighton trains. Because their valves were small in relation to the cylinders, the engines were not 'flyers' in the Great Western sense and one able driver showed that a fixed regulator opening and fixed cut-off setting could suffice to keep time over 36 miles of 1 in 264 undulations without excessive downhill speeds (Bib. 31).

Great Western 2/2-6-2Ts were multiplied extensively, but the LMS decided that a tank engine should be able to complete a whole day's work without refilling the coal bunker and on that account adopted the 2/2-6-4T rather than the 2/2-6-2T. Ironically, this happened in 1927 when high-speed derailments of 2/2-6-4Ts on the Southern decided that group never to use such locomotives on passenger trains. But there was no particular trouble on the LMS, and 2/2-6-4Ts built by the LMS, the LNE, and BR numbered over 800.

Able to run up to 90 mph and to develop 1,000 drawbar horsepower for short periods, the LMS 2/2-6-4Ts were very useful locomotives. It must be added that very few regular tank-engine duties ever called for such speed or power. A great many of the 2-6-4Ts ran for weeks on end without pulling any train so heavy as the engine. The Great Western had enough small tank engines to enable it to avoid such wasteful work.

Perhaps the most enlivening report about Great Western 0-4-2Ts is that one was timed at very nearly 80 mph when pushing a single coach from Stonehouse to Gloucester (Bib. 6).

High power output in relation to size was unusual in tank engines and only one such effort is represented in Appendix 3. This was by No 1532, a LY superheated 2-4-2T (R149) pulling the 4.25 PM Salford-Colne up the 1 in 78 of Helm-shore bank (Bib. 7).

Many tank engines spent most of their time on menial but essential work. For example, ex-LSW M7 tank engines (R146) brought empty trains into Waterloo Station and helped them out again. Without such help the Southern 'Pacifics' could have paralysed the working of Waterloo by their uncertainty in starting with heavy trains.

CHANGE ON THE NORTH WESTERN

Webb's rule over the locomotive department of the London & North Western Railway was something like that of Hitler in Germany. No one dared to hint at any imperfection in the head man's methods. So everyone carried on as best he could with hordes of wretched compound engines and everyone knew what sort of engines would have done the work easily. It needed no imagination, as the North Western simple engines (many of Webb's design) did their work well. They were not particularly economical but they were reliable and could stand hard work.

So, as soon as Webb retired, his successor, Whale, gave the word to the drawing-office and something useful was soon on the way. The best North Western passenger engines were the 2-4-0 'Jumbos' and the best goods engines were the 0-6-0 'Cauliflowers'. Something bigger was required and Crewe produced the 4-4-0 'Precursor' (R11) which had an enlarged version of the boiler used by the six-wheel engines. The engine proper was similar to that of the 'Cauliflowers' in having inside cylinders with flat valves on top, Joy valve gear, and a third axlebox between the cranks on the leading coupled axle. The deep firebox was easy to fire and the engines were as foolproof as the large 'Atlantics' on the Great Northern.

Because of the climbs from sea level at Carnforth and

Carlisle to the 900-ft high summit at Shap, it was thought that a six-coupled passenger engine was needed for the North Western main line north of Crewe. So the 4-6-0 'Experiment' (R29) was produced with slightly smaller coupled wheels than the 4-4-0, packed together into almost the same total wheelbase. The cylinders and valves were the same in both classes, but the fireboxes were quite different because the grate on the 4-6-0 had to be above the two rear coupled axles, some 2 ft higher than on the 4-4-0 although the boiler centre heights were about the same. The shallow firebox was

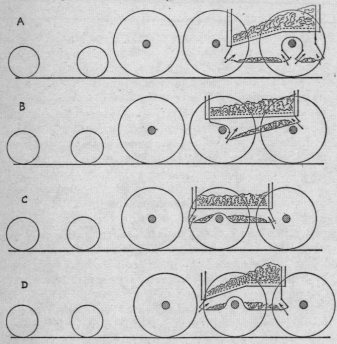

7. Fireboxes and ashpans on some 4-6-0s

A – GW R37-41 R65-67   C – LNW R29 R30 R31
B – LSW T14 R73   D – GE '1500' R34

longer than the deep one and was very much more difficult to fire, because the front end of it had to be kept supplied with no aid from gravity and with little clearance under the brick arch. The inevitable result was that average performance of the 4-6-0s was well below that of the 4-4-0s although a good fireman really doing his best could make an 'Experiment' show the advantage over a 'Precursor' that the bigger grate might have been expected to give it.

In later years, Bowen-Cooke fitted many of the 'Precursors' with superheaters, new cylinders with piston valves, and smaller bogie wheels and they were then identical (except for a detail in the splashers) with the 'George V' class. No 'Experiment' was similarly converted, although the 'Prince of Wales' class, which was a superheated version of the 'Experiments', eventually numbered 245 engines.

The Whale engines and their superheated successors were plain, straightforward locomotives with no pretence of refinement or of anything specially progressive in their design. They were needed quickly, they were produced quickly and even when over-loaded, as became normal, they played their part in establishing for the North Western a high reputation for punctuality. They were painted black with grey and red lining, they had unobtrusive name-plates, dignified number-plates but no lettering whatever on the side sheets of the tenders. The black paint, in contrast to the colours used for passenger engines on all the other large British railways except the LY, had earned for Webb's engines the name of 'flying hearses' and it was probably only the black paint that led some unsophisticated observer to suggest many years later that they were a 'rough job'.

Bowen-Cooke first applied superheating to North Western locomotives under the instructions of Dr Schmidt (developer of the firetube superheater in Germany) not only in respect of the superheater itself but also of associated details. He applied a single broad ring to each piston-valve head; this worked, but not for long without serious leakage. By 1913 the Knorr

Brake Co were making piston valves with the multiple narrow rings invented by Ramsbottom at Crewe sixty years earlier and adopted by the LMS for piston valves twenty years later.

The broad conception of the 4/4-6-0 'Claughton' (R68) was excellent, but some of its details showed a sad lack of grasp of basic essentials and of appreciation of practical requirements. Application of real understanding to the design could have made the 'Claughtons' distinctive performers throughout the remaining history of steam.

CHANGE ON THE GREAT WESTERN

The change in design policy on the North Western in 1904 was largely a panic measure. The corresponding change on the Great Western in 1900–05 was anything but that. It was a carefully reasoned process based on the anticipated needs of the Great Western for twenty-five years ahead. Main-line passenger engines, goods engines, and tank engines were considered simultaneously so that all requirements could be covered by the smallest possible number of different designs of boilers, cylinders, motion, and wheels. Outside cylinders were adopted to avoid the cost of crank axles, and Stephenson valve gear was standardized. The standard boilers had high Belpaire fireboxes, in gentled imitation of the old 'haystack' fireboxes, with tapered barrels to reduce weight at the front end where nothing is lost by making the diameter less than it is at the firebox.

Where long-term standardization is being studied it is specially important to examine every detail of design and this was done at Swindon. Even to a casual observer the appearance of the Churchward engines was markedly un-English, but there were many less noticeable, and indeed invisible, features that departed importantly from convention.

One of these was the provision of adequate water-spaces round the firebox. In British practice a width of $2\frac{1}{4}$ ins was common, but even 2 ins was used, and there were some instances of 3 ins. The Swindon standard was 3½ ins and this was made clear in a paper read by Churchward before the Institution of Mechanical Engineers in 1906.

Churchward's most important departure from convention was the provision of valves large enough to enable the cylinders to use the full steam output of the boiler with the highest efficiency (ie, with cut-off between 15 and 25 per cent) at the maximum sustained running speed expected of the class concerned. Flat valves of the period were too small for this, as indeed were many piston valves also, but Churchward published dimensions of the steam ports in his standard engines so that everyone could see what he was doing. It was impossible, in any case, to make any secret of his developments in this respect, as an interested observer had only to look at the size of the steam chest, to see how far the valve-spindle moved when the engine started away in 'full gear' and to hear the sound of the exhaust to realize that this was something new in British practice.

Churchward adopted as standard the American practice of using a cylindrical smokebox resting on a saddle instead of the usual awkward wrapper-plate connexion with the cylinder casting. Most British engineers resolutely refused to adopt anything so practical and even as late as 1927 the new LMS 'Royal Scots' were built with wrapper-plate smokeboxes.

But more important than the details of mounting the smokebox was the dimensioning of the things inside it. To obtain high efficiency in a locomotive the chimney, petticoat-pipe, blast-pipe, and smokebox had to be designed to create the necessary draught through the fire with the minimum steam pressure in the blast-pipe and therefore minimum back pressure on the pistons. The value of good design of the 'front end' had long been recognized and the American Master Mechanics Association had adopted, as standard, formulae recommended by Professor Goss of Purdue University for the dimensions of front-ends. Churchward based his designs on Goss proportions, slightly modified after experimental adjustments, and nothing better is known. But the misplaced ingenuity applied by other British locomotive engineers in producing front-ends markedly different from the well-tried Goss style was almost pathetic. In time, however, they all came round to it.

One quite unnoticeable feature of Churchward design was an axlebox that was far less likely to overheat than were most others then and for thirty years afterwards. The main point here was to avoid cutting any oil-groove in the top part of the cylindrical surface that pressed on the axle.

Practices that did affect the outward appearance were the collecting of steam in the high leading corners of the outer firebox instead of in a dome, the use of direct-loaded safety valves in a conical brass cover that made 'blowing-off' noise less noticeable to people near the engine, and the feeding of water to the boiler through clack valves attached to the safety-valve mounting.

Old Great Western features that were retained on all the new Churchward designs were the copper-capped chimney (except during World War I and for a few years afterwards), brass-edged splashers, and cast-brass number-plates. The 'trimmings' were early-Victorian but the essential guts were second-Elizabethan.

A broad plan drawn up by Churchward in 1901 envisaged 2/4-6-0, 2/2-8-0 and 2/2-6-2T designs with many components common to all. Ten years later Swindon produced 2/2-6-0s and 2/2-8-0Ts not contemplated in 1901, but nevertheless built almost entirely from components of the original standard designs.

Churchward's work, unique in the history of the British steam locomotive, was the development of entirely new standard designs of boilers, cylinders, wheels, and mechanism, making sure that air, water, steam, and flue-gases would have adequate freedom of profitable movement through the locomotive, that wasteful leakage was eliminated, and that all

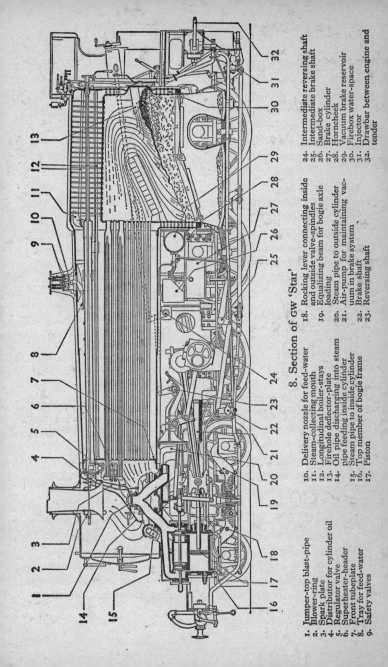

8. Section of GW 'Star'

1. Jumper-top blast-pipe
2. Blower-ring
3. Spark plate
4. Distributor for cylinder oil
5. Regulator valve
6. Superheater-header
7. Front tubeplate
8. Tray for feed-water
9. Safety valves
10. Delivery nozzle for feed-water
11. Steam-collecting mouth
12. Longitudinal boiler-stays
13. Firehole deflector-plate
14. Oil pipe discharging into steam pipe feeding inside cylinder
15. Steam pipe to inside cylinder
16. Top member of bogie frame
17. Piston
18. Rocking lever connecting inside and outside valve-spindles
19. Equalizing beam for bogie axle loading
20. Steam pipe to outside cylinder
21. Air-pump for maintaining vacuum in brake system
22. Brake shaft
23. Reversing shaft
24. Intermediate reversing shaft
25. Intermediate brake shaft
26. Sand-box
27. Brake cylinder
28. Horncheek
29. Vacuum brake reservoir
30. Firebox water-space
31. Injector
32. Drawbar between engine and tender

working parts were big enough to do their jobs over long life with little attention in service. These components sufficed as the basic constituents of a dozen classes of Great Western locomotives, introduced at various times over a period of forty years. (On the other hand there was little of Churchward design in the hundreds of o-6-oPTs built for the Great Western after 1928).

A very remarkable feature of the Churchward two-cylinder engines was that each cylinder was made in one piece with half the smokebox saddle and the combination was bolted to an extension of the frame. Either cylinder and half-saddle (or both) could be taken away without removing the boiler which could remain partly supported by a second saddle formed as an upward extension of the motion plate.

When Churchward retired at the end of 1922 he had so well anticipated Great Western needs that Swindon design had no need to depart from the general principles he had developed. His 'Star' class 4/4-6-0 (R65) was non-standard in having four cylinders and inside valve gear very hard to reach. Its outside cylinders were attached to the frame plates at their weakest place and heavy cross-bracing was necessary. But the self-balancing tendency of four cylinders enabled the engines to run smoothly at high speed, and the design was adopted by Churchward's successor in its enlarged forms of 'Castle' (R66) and 'King' (R67).

There were, however, some grievous defects in Swindon practice. The cabs of the tender engines were very draughty and uncomfortable. It was common to pull a heavy flap-plate up in front of the firehole after each shovelful of coal and to pull it down again before the next, whereas a sensible firedoor could give the same result with a tenth of the labour. In Collett's time, two-cylinder engines running fast battered the track with colossal balance-weights specially provided to diminish pulsation of pull of the train at low speeds, whereas reduction in pre-load of the drawbar spring was all that was necessary.

But comparable faults could be found on every railway!

CHAPTER THREE

SOME CONSTRUCTIONAL FEATURES

Boilers

THERE WAS never any successful departure in steam-locomotive practice from the general form of the multi-tubular boiler used on Stephenson's *Planet* of 1830. There were, however, several alternative configurations of the firebox end of it.

The first British railway to use a Belpaire firebox (eg, p 61) was the Manchester, Sheffield & Lincolnshire, later extended to form the Great Central which continued that construction in every boiler. Before 1914 it had been adopted by most lines in England, except the Great Northern and the North Eastern. It was a feature of the standard designs on the Great Western and later on the LMS. By presenting a flat crown of the outer firebox to the corresponding sheet of the inner firebox it admitted of simpler stays than those required with a round-top firebox.

The only advantage of the taper boiler barrel used on the Great Western, and later on the LMS, was a small reduction in weight at the front and a small reduction in the change in level of the water over the firebox with a sudden large change in gradient of the rails. These differences might just be perceptible in a large locomotive and there the taper might improve the driver's view of the track ahead.

Thermic Syphon

This made a marked addition to the firebox heating surface in the form of a pipe and double-wall triangle forming a path

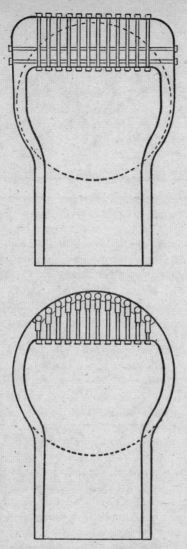

9. Cross-section of fireboxes, Belpaire and round-topped

for water from the front of the firebox to the roof. It was tried by the North Western and by the LNE but its only extensive use in Britain was in Southern 'Pacifics'. It justified itself only at higher combustion rates than were usual in Britain. It was probably an important factor in the remarkable performances of Chapelon locomotives in France but it showed no advantage in the Southern 'Pacific' tested by British Railways at Rugby.

Valves and valve gear (pp 12 and 13).

Stephenson valve gear was the most widely used form in Great Britain before 1914, but Walschaerts gear was being adopted and after grouping it was applied to almost all outside valves except on the Great Western where Stephenson gear was standard for two-cylinder engines.

Joy valve gear was used very extensively on the LNW and the LY but not elsewhere. It was well suited to valves above inside cylinders but it was driven by the connecting-rod and the design was not in every case adequate for long and trouble-free service.

A great many different forms of valve gear were invented and some of them were tried for short periods. But Walschaerts gear (invented about 1840) gradually became a world standard.

The basic dimension of a flat valve or of a piston valve was the 'lap', in the nineteenth century, about an inch, boldly replaced by about 1·7 ins by Churchward in 1903 and slowly increased in small, reluctant and protesting steps by other designers to that figure in about thirty years.

The 'lead' (the opening of the valve when the piston was at the end of the stroke) might be anything from nothing to about 0·3 ins, and quite dramatic improvements in performance of the locomotive were sometimes attributed to minute changes in this dimension. Every such claim needed very critical examination in view of circumstances illustrated by the remark of an American locomotive engineer that the coal consumption of any engine could be reduced by 25 per cent simply by painting the chimney blue. He meant that if anything suggested to the enginemen that the performance of their engine was being specially watched, they would (where there was anything like discipline) immediately begin to do all the things that they were supposed to have been doing and this sufficed to transform performance.

In many circumstances build-up of carbon in ports in a few thousand miles so reduced port openings that to talk of sixteenths of an inch in connexion with lap or lead was laughable.

Compound expansion

Expansion of steam, in successive stages, in different cylinders in a steam locomotive had the sole advantage that the fall in temperature of the steam in any one cylinder was less than that in a single cylinder in which the whole expansion was effected. This meant a reduction in the chilling effect on live steam of the ports just previously swept by exhaust steam cooled during expansion. In favourable circumstances compounding in a steam locomotive might save 5 to 10 per cent in coal, but against this had to be set increased maintenance cost if the compound engine had more than two cylinders, as most of them did.

Many British railways tried compounding but only the Midland was sufficiently impressed to retain it in a numerous class for top-rank passenger trains.

Worthwhile economy from compounding in a steam locomotive would demand a boiler pressure of at least 700 psi. This is far beyond the economic limit of the conventional locomotive boiler and no other type of boiler has had any real success at all in a locomotive. The LNE 4C/4-6-4 with 450 psi water-tube boiler exemplified this in 1930–32.

Poppet Valves

Independent control by poppet valves of admission of steam
to cylinders, and its subsequent exhaust, gave much more
scope in designing valve events than could be obtained from
a piston valve because that exerted its own correlation of
admission and exhaust. It happened, however, that that
correlation did not prohibit design for highest cylinder
efficiency.

Poppet valves, having no heavily loaded sliding surfaces,
could be worked with a fraction of the power required for the
corresponding piston valves, which themselves were superior
in this respect to flat valves. But as even those valves need take
only about 2 per cent of the power developed in the cylinders,
the scope for advantage from poppet valves in this respect
was very narrow indeed.

Poppet valves cost less in maintenance than did piston
valves but even these were not expensive.

Poppet valves were tried in many countries with enthusiasm in successive waves, one of which was rising here
when the last British steam locomotives were being built.

Multiple exhaust

The simple blast-pipe and chimney in a British locomotive
could be designed (with perhaps some readjustment after
trial) for any output up to 2,000-indicated horsepower at
combustion rates in the usual British range with a blast-
pipe pressure of about 5 psi. The only possible economy of
any alternative was to reduce that 5 psi; there was not much
room for improvement nor was much ever shown.

But if a much higher combustion rate were required,
stronger draught was necessary and, to produce it, blast-
pipe pressure might have to be raised to perhaps 10 psi.
To make full use of this with the simple blast-pipe and chimney the ideal distance between them might be too much for

the available height. In that case two blast-pipes and chimneys of smaller diameters might be used, as the ideal distance between them might thus be brought into the available range.

Similarly, if say 3,000-indicated horsepower were required even at a conventional combustion rate, the ideal single blast-pipe and chimney might require more height than was available; there again the difficulty could be avoided by using a double chimney.

In neither case was there any harm (or advantage) in subdividing the exhaust even further or in inserting petti-coat-pipes. No such artifice ever showed any perceptible advantage over the plain blast-pipe and chimney ideally designed for the conditions but of course it might, and some-times did, show advantage over a badly designed version of the conventional scheme.

One such artifice (the Giesl ejector) did, however, have an advantage of a quite different kind. Its nozzle and chimney were only a few inches wide and so it minimized obstruction to the recurrent operation of cleaning tubes. Very regrettably, British Railways, against all the protestations of the technical staff who were quite clear on the matter, were misguided into spending taxpayers' money on comparative tests on a 2/2-10-0 of class 9 in the vain hope of disproving French and German findings that the advantage of the Giesl ejector over a properly designed double chimney was too uncertain to be worth bothering about (Bib. 37, p 141).

For a particular combustion rate in a particular locomotive the only possible advantage of one exhaust system over another was in reduced back pressure on the pistons; the bigger the pistons the bigger the advantage. This meant, that for a given nominal tractive effort, the lower the boiler pressure the bigger the advantage to be gained. Yet most multiple-exhaust systems in Britain were applied to loco-motives with 250-psi boiler pressure; few if any were used with 180-psi pressure, where their advantage would have been

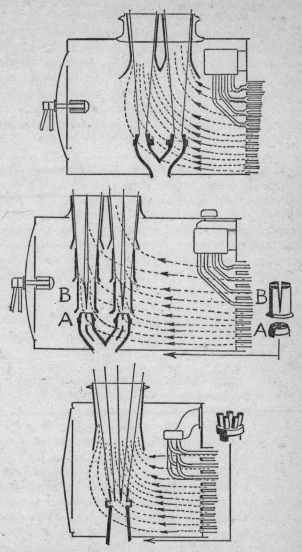

10A. Double chimney (eg, LMS 'Rebuilt Scot')
10B. Kylchap double exhaust (eg, some LNE 'Pacifics')
10C. Lemaître multiple exhaust and wide chimney (eg, some SR 'Schools')

40 per cent greater although, even at that, not substantial.

Locomotives would often show themselves to be much more powerful in service after being fitted with double blast-pipes (or the like) than they were before and this naturally suggested that the altered arrangement was getting more work out of the coal. In fact, it was merely that the quietness of the multiple exhaust induced the driver to work the engine harder than he normally did. The fireman knew that they were burning more coal per mile and the test engineers knew that they were getting hardly any more work out of each pound of coal.

Because even the highest powers and combustion rates required in Britain were within the capacity of a single blast-pipe without unduly high blast-pipe pressure, multiple-exhaust systems were not extensively used in this country before World War II. Imperfections in coal and maintenance during the war, and after it, gave more scope for multiple exhaust, and it became more widely applied. In Appendix 2, only those classes originally built with multiple exhaust are marked with A, K, or L after the figure for grate area.

Front-end (*Smokebox and internal fittings*)

Over the years the smokebox changed in shape from a biscuit towards a sausage. The first positive move in this direction was made on the Great Western as a means of reducing the throwing of sparks by hard-working engines. It was a copy of American practice whereby the gases that came out of the tubes were deflected towards the lower half of the smokebox door. Thence the gases were drawn back and up by the blast, but the larger solid particles were unable to make the quick turn and so struck the door and fell to the bottom of the box. This arrangement (p 58) demanded that the chimney be well ahead of the tubeplate and that the front of the smokebox be well ahead of the chimney. Unless the smokebox were of generous length, either the lower

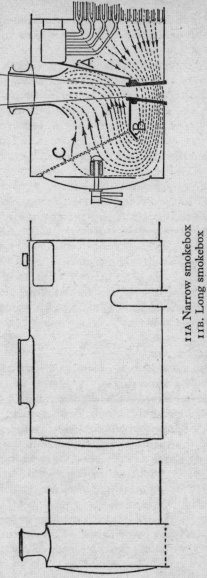

11A Narrow smokebox
11B. Long smokebox
11C. Self-cleaning smokebox

tubes tended to become blocked, thus impairing the production of steam, or many sparks were thrown out of the chimney.

Where the chimney was near the front of a long smokebox the reason was usually that the blast-pipe had been placed as close as possible to the cylinders while the position of the tubeplate had been determined by the desired length of tubes.

Although good front-end proportions derived from Goss researches were published in 1904, nobody in Britain except Churchward took any immediate notice of them. One consequence was that over forty years later Swindon could take a locomotive from some other group than the Great Western and add 50 per cent or so to its steaming capacity simply by fitting it with different blast-pipe and petticoat-pipe – which the original designer might have specified if he had made the best use of available information.

The old method of making the smokebox is based on the use of a 'wrapper-plate' bent into the form of about three-quarters of a cylinder with parallel prolongations that are bolted to the frame or the cylinder casting. The front tubeplate and its downward extension are riveted to the wrapper-plate and also bolted to the cylinder casting. It is an awkward construction and there was often much trouble in trying to maintain the airtight joints that are necessary for full power or highest efficiency.

In the early years of the century Churchward standardized the American 'drumhead' tubeplate with a cylindrical smokebox that is bolted to a saddle shaped to receive it. This construction is superior to the older one in every way but prolonged resistance to its adoption was shown by many British railways. Everybody knew that the wrapper-type smokebox was a pest, but it always had been, so why worry? As late as 1927, for example, the LMS 'Royal Scot' design repeated the wrapper-type of smokebox and it proved to be a perennial weak point in a generally good engine.

Boiler pressure

From 50 psi in Stephenson's *Rocket*, locomotive boiler pressures had risen to a general average of about 180 psi in 1900 and no advantage was obtainable in the conventional steam locomotive from deliberately adopting anything higher. A designer might, however, be forced to go higher in order to attain the desired nominal tractive effort in the largest cylinders that he could fit in. But raising the designed pressure of a boiler meant that it had to be made stronger and therefore heavier. If it were already at the limit of allowable weight, a higher pressure meant that it would have to be smaller. Moreover, every increase in working pressure meant increase in maintenance cost and it was generally agreed that, on this account, 300 psi was the limit for the conventional locomotive boiler.

Superheating

Expansion of steam cools it and, if it has come straight from the boiler, cooling condenses it. If the steam is made hotter after leaving the boiler it can suffer some cooling before it begins to condense. By applying sufficient 'superheat' to the steam on its way from the boiler to the cylinders, condensation in the cylinders is eliminated and this reduces the coal consumption by about 25 per cent. A higher degree of superheating serves no purpose but to save water which is not usually important. Superheating makes cylinder lubrication more difficult and the hotter the steam the worse it is.

Churchward made the heating surface of the superheater about 10 times the grate area and if the flues were kept clean this produced all the superheat that was any good. But to attain the same result with flues partly blocked with cinders, a large superheater was necessary and British practice tended to a ratio of 15 rather than 10.

Gresley tried 25 in a very large superheater fitted to a

'Pacific' and found, as Churchward could have foretold him, no advantage from it.

Firegrate

Most of the early steam locomotives had deep fireboxes with firegrates parallel to the rails. In some cases the grate sloped down from back to front and, at the turn of the century, 4-4-0s had begun to be built with boilers of which the rear end was above and behind the rear axle, the firebox thus being shallow at the back but reasonably deep at the front by virtue of a sloping grate.

Many 4-6-0s had grates that were horizontal in the back half but sloped in the front half, but some (eg, SR 'King Arthurs') were sloped throughout; the original North Western 'Claughton' boilers had partly sloped grates but continuous slope was provided in later boilers. An appropriate slope eased the fireman's work by combining with vibration to induce the fire-bed to shuffle slowly down to the front.

Some slope was usually given to grates in wide fireboxes and in the LMS 'Pacifics' the grate was less wide at the back than at the front, so as to reduce the difficulty of feeding the back corners through the single central firehole.

Grates were usually composed of single steel firebars lowered into position from inside the firebox. A 'drop grate' that could be swung down to discharge unwanted fire into the ashpan was used as early as 1852 but the drop grate did not become a standard fitting on any British locomotive till Gresley applied it to his first 'Pacifics' in 1922. He used it also in other LNE standard classes but the practice spread only very slowly elsewhere in Great Britain.

A 'rocking and dumping' grate was one composed of short firebars that could be rocked in groups by levers on the footplate in order to break up clinker or to shuffle fine ash into the ashpan, or could be given a bigger angular displacement from the normal position so that all the fire dropped

through. Grates of this type were fitted to some LMS locomotives built in World War II, and certain BR standard
classes also had them.

Self-cleaning smokebox

Many locomotive smokeboxes were at one time or another
fitted with large pipes through which the accumulated 'char'
could be discharged on to the track between the rails, thus
avoiding one shovelling operation. Such devices did not
persist in Britain, possibly because their full value could be
secured only if the next movement of the char were equally
well organized as, for example, by discharging from the
smokebox into wheeled containers below track level.

American 2-8-0s brought into Britain during World War II
introduced here the 'self-cleaning smokebox' (p 68) designed
to eject from the chimney all but the largest pieces of solid
matter that reached the smokebox. This was done by lower-
ing the front edge of the diaphragm so as to increase the
speed of the gases to the point that impelled all solid matter
to rise in the front half of the smokebox and so to reach the
chimney after passing through a wire net that stopped only the
biggest pieces. The adoption of this scheme usually demanded
some readjustment of blast-pipe orifice to cope with the extra
draught resistance. It was effective in saving labour at the
engine shed but at the cost of extra work for those housewives
who dried their washing alongside the railway.

The same effect could be produced in all North Western
locomotives built after about 1880. Whenever he chose, the
fireman could direct steam into perforated pipes in the
bottom of the smokebox. The issuing steam so agitated the
fine cinders there that they became caught up in the draught
and the blast shot them out of the chimney, to fall audibly on
the train.

Ashpan

The ashpan was a steel box attached to the underside of the firebox, for the purpose of catching cinders, ash, and anything else that might fall out of the fire through the spaces between the firebars.

The ashpan was fitted with horizontally hinged flaps ('dampers') that could be set to adjust the widths of openings through which air gained admission over the ash to the underside of the fire.

Where the firebox was placed over an axle, the ashpan had to be specially shaped to clear the axle (see p 53) and in that vicinity the pan might be very close to the firebars.

Not every designer realized that the fire could be throttled by build-up of ash in the ashpan or that full use of the firegrate required easy access of air to every part of its underside. Some 4-6-os were very bad in this respect.

The ashpan could be the 'bottleneck' in the design of a locomotive required to develop high power over more than about 250 miles with no opportunity for emptying the ashpan. In this respect the 'Garratt' locomotive had a big advantage.

Injectors

The normal method of feeding water into a locomotive boiler was by the 'injector' in which the energy of a jet of steam from the boiler was used to develop such pressure in feedwater as to enable it to force its way into the boiler.

By using part of the exhaust steam to heat and pressurize feedwater on its way to the injector, coal consumption could be reduced by about 7 per cent. Such 'exhaust-steam injectors' were used as early as 1900 and were considerably developed before World War I. They were, however, much more sensitive to adverse conditions (maladjustment and solid matter in the water) even than plain injectors and they earned so much disfavour on this account during World War II that they were specifically excluded from British Railways standard locomotives.

Steam Passages

Much of the work of a high-speed locomotive could be done without appreciable loss of efficiency with the boiler pressure down to 70 per cent of the rated maximum and, indeed, many locomotives were purposely worked on the level and downhill with steam-chest pressure as low as that.

Drop of steam pressure between the boiler and the steam chests does not mean loss of energy; there is nowhere for it to escape unless indeed there is leakage of steam. The thermal gain from making steam pipes straight instead of curved and from polishing the walls of steam passages was purely imaginary. There were three sharp reverse bends in every superheater element and while they remained there was no object in bothering about a few slight bends · elsewhere. Steam ports were usually coated with oily carbon for most of their lives however well they may have been polished in manufacture, as was said to have been done in some cases.

The really important ideal about what was sometimes unaccountably described as the 'steam circuit' was that there should be no leak anywhere and especially not into the smokebox, because there it could markedly reduce the draught on the fire.

Steam-lifting

When a locomotive was running fast, air struck by the smoke-box emerged radially from its front edge and created a partial vacuum immediately behind the edge. Forward flow of air along the surface of the smokebox to fill this vacuum produced an annular vortex all round the edge. If the chimney were very short, steam and smoke from it were drawn forwards into the vortex and might escape from it in a downward direction. The steam that flowed backwards from a short chimney often clung to the surface of the boiler and obscured the front windows of the cab. Considerable difficulty was experienced on this account when running with low exhaust pressure and the Southern 'King Arthurs' were among the first British offenders although the LMS 'Royal Scots' were probably the worst. Many efforts were made with small steel plates and alterations to smokeboxes to overcome this trouble but the only substantial success was achieved by large vertical plates that gave an upward trend to the air that would otherwise have spread sideways from the edge of the smokebox. Brought from Germany by the Southern Railway in 1927 this method of smoke-lifting was accepted as the best solution to the problem. After many years of use of this device it was found that, on some locomotives at least, it was effective with plates very much smaller than those used in its earliest applications.

Cabs and Cab-fittings

In 1900 the cabs on most British locomotives afforded the enginemen so little protection against the weather as not to justify the name 'cab'. Exceptions occurred on the North Eastern where side-window cabs had been common in new construction for some fifteen years and on the Great Eastern where side-window cabs had been applied to the 'Claud Hamilton' 4-4-0s and were standard in subsequent designs. On the North British, also, side-window cabs were soon to be adopted.

With these exceptions there was no general move to design new locomotives with reasonably protective cabs. Even then, efforts in this direction were not appreciated as enclosed cabs were uncomfortably hot in warm weather and might make it difficult to handle long fire-irons. They were, moreover, apt to be noisy unless very heavily built and some BR standard cabs were much criticized on this account.

Gresley used V-fronted cabs on his standard 2-6-2s (R129) with some very slight advantage in reduced wind resistance at high speeds but with the disadvantage of excessive internal heat because of enclosing an abnormally large part of the top of the boiler. The claim that the V-front cab avoided reflection of internal light by the front windows after dark was somewhat forced, as there was no difficulty in fitting angled front windows in a flat-fronted cab.

Front windows tended to be quickly obscured by emissions from the chimney and, unless made to open inwards, could not be easily cleaned from inside the cab. On this account much use was made of narrow glass strips projecting from the cab-sides immediately in front of the side openings, as such strips could easily be cleaned. They were introduced to Great Britain by the Great Western 4-6-0 'King George V' on returning from a visit to America in 1927 and were adopted by the other three groups. The Great Western, on the other hand, rejected the scheme because the front windows on most Great Western engines opened inwards and Great Western enginemen normally leaned out of the cab only to get a cool breeze in hot weather.

Side doors appreciably reduced the draught on a footplate, particularly when a side wind was blowing, but because of the relative motion of engine and tender they could not be made anything like airtight. (On a tank engine matters were easier.) So some railways (eg, the Great Western) never used them on tender engines. Ivatt 'Atlantics' had doors that swung inwards to give free passage but were fixed, in running, with the rear edges outside the cab outline with the hope that the inclination of the face of the door to the direction of the relative wind would cause it to extract air from the cab, just as the ejector extracted air from the train pipe.

Many Scottish locomotives engaged on goods trains and in shunting had 'home-made' side doors apparently built by nailing together scrap ends of wooden planks.

With increase in boiler diameter, cabs became wider and many were so near to the limit of the loading gauge that there was no room for the running-board to project sufficiently to provide a foothold, and so the men could not get ahead of the cab while the engine was running. There was normally no need to do so, but it was the only way of escape from a cab filled with flame or steam as the result of a failure of a fire-tube or boiler fitting. The tender was no sure refuge even if there were room in it, as the draught of forward running spread the dangers of the cab in that direction. American practice mitigated this difficulty with an emergency brake handle in the tender. Some features of British practice suggested that as accidents of this character were rare (especially to designers!) it was superfluous to take them into account.

Firedoor design had been traditional on each railway and the men became used to what was provided however bad it might be. Thus Great Northern, Great Central, and LNE practice was to use a shallow, roughly rectangular opening bisected by a 'butterfly' plate on a horizontal axis at mid-depth, cutting down the usable height of opening to about 6 ins but leaving another 6 ins open for entry by an excessive amount of cold air. All this was contained in a door that might be opened to expose the full firehole which was a circle about 18 ins in diameter.

The most widely used form of firedoor was in two halves, movable horizontally by linkage with a single handle. Great Western practice provided in addition a flap-plate swung up about a horizontal axis under the door by a pull on a chain after each shovelful of coal was fired.

It was usually valuable, and sometimes essential, to keep the door closed for every instant that was not required for in-sertion of coal, and a power-operated firedoor controlled by a treadle was an American scheme introduced to Great Britain by Bulleid on his Southern 'Pacifics' of 1941. But the treadle was not convenient to work (you had to stand on one foot) and when in need of adustment the mechanism might suddenly close the door and endanger the fireman's hands. For that reason some firemen declined to use it.

It seems, in any case, ponderously elaborate to use steam power to move a plate away from a hole. It was, in fact, possible to make a firedoor that opened by gravity when a pawl was disengaged from a notch by horizontal pressure of the sole of the fireman's shoe upon a detent on the cab floor, and that was restored to its normal (closed) position by lifting it with the shovel.

Matters of this sort were apparently ignored by designers and even some of those directly concerned were not well informed. On some railways it was normal practice for the driver to open and close the firedoor before and after each shot by the fireman when the maximum power output was required, whereas enginemen on other railways had never heard of it.

Wide variations were to be seen in the relation between the position of the firehole and that of the plate from which coal is shovelled out of the tender. The ideal horizontal distance was about 5 ft, leaving room for the fireman to swing the shovel without banging his hands on anything hard and yet not demanding a big stretch to reach either coal or hole, but anything from 3 ft to 8 ft could be found in British locomotives. The ideal difference in height between plate and door is zero; there were many labour-making departures from this, but British Railways standard designs had it, and so did those of Stroudley, seventy years earlier. A difficulty here in the case of a large locomotive was that of finding room for an adequate self-trimming supply of coal above firehole level.

The footplate should ideally extend far enough backwards for the fireman to do his work without standing on the fall-plate between the engine and tender. Great Eastern engines had this feature and it was included in British Railways standard designs.

It was not easy to find room for all the necessary and desirable cab fittings without restricting the view of the crew through the front windows. The Southern 'Pacifics' were not ideal in this respect.

On many engines the brake handle was so far from the side of the cab that the driver could not reach it when he was leaning out to see the vehicle up to which he was backing the engine. This inconvenience was avoidable by providing a brake-application valve on the end of a $1\frac{1}{4}$-in pipe clipped to the side of the cab, where it could also be reached from outside by anyone driven from the footplate by accidental intrusion of fire, steam or hot water. Certain North Western 'coal tank' 0-6-2Ts had a flap valve in this position on a pipe connecting the ejector with the train pipe but this was quite exceptional. On contemporary Midland 0-4-4Ts the brake-application handle was at about knee-height above the footplate.

When superheating was new, each engine might be provided with a pyrometer to indicate the temperature of the superheated steam, but this information was not specially valuable in ordinary service and is certainly not necessary. So pyrometers were abandoned in World War I and did not reappear.

Steam-chest pressure gauges were similarly superfluous and indeed even the absence of a boiler-pressure gauge did not prevent a locomotive from being used as, in any event, reliance was placed on the safety valves to avoid the one dangerous consequence of enginemen's ignorance of the boiler pressure.

Some confident characters would keep going even when failure of gauge glasses left them with no direct indication of water-level in the boiler but most drivers would stop the job with far less encouragement than that.

CHAPTER FOUR

MORE THAN TWO CYLINDERS

THE EARLIEST steam locomotives and the latest steam locomotives had only two cylinders each. What justification was there for using more than two cylinders in any locomotive? The answers are:

1. The possibility of balancing the reciprocating parts so that the hammer-blow on the track was much smaller than for a two-cylinder locomotive of equal power and so that vibration in the locomotive itself was small.
2. The possibility of providing a much greater total cylinder volume and therefore of obtaining any desired nominal tractive effort with lower boiler pressure than would otherwise be necessary and therefore with a lighter boiler of any specified major dimensions.
3. The possibility of setting the cranks so as to obtain a smaller variation of tractive effort and a smaller variation of draught on the fire during each revolution of the driving wheels than was possible with only two cylinders.

The disadvantages of using more than two cylinders were:

(a) Extra cost in construction and maintenance.
(b) Greater weight of mechanism for any specified power.
(c) Greater loss in friction.

Advantage 1 was obtained automatically. Only deliberately absurd design could avoid it.

Advantage 2 does not seem to have been generally recognized although there is one example that demonstrates it clearly. On the LMS, the 'Royal Scot' of 1927 was followed three years later by the so-called 'Baby Scot' working at

200 psi instead of 250 in a slightly smaller boiler. The lighter 'Baby' was allowed to run on routes prohibited to the 'Royal Scots' which were sufficiently numerous to cover the West Coast main-line services, but there was little to choose between the two classes in performance.

Advantage 3 is perceptible only when the locomotive is pulling hard at very low speed. In a two-cylinder locomotive or a four-cylinder locomotive with cranks at right angles (four beats per revolution) the maximum pull was about 10 per cent higher than the mean pull. For three cylinders the figure was 5 per cent. For four cylinders with cranks at 0, 45, 90, and 135 degrees (eight beats per revolution) the figure was 2 per cent.

The 'strengths' of individual beats of exhaust steam at the blast-pipe were roughly in the ratio of 1, 0·7, and 0·5 for the three arrangements, but the variation of draught on the fire itself became much less than this as the interval of time between successive beats was reduced. All these differences were markedly reduced at any driving-wheel speed higher than about one revolution per second.

The eight-beat principle applied to 'Claughton' 4-6-0s on the LMS showed no advantage whatever over four beats. One of the Southern 'Lord Nelsons' was altered from eight beats to four as one of a number of attempts to improve performance.

Disadvantages (*b*) and (*c*) did not prevent multi-cylinder locomotives from showing high efficiency (Appendix 4), high power in relation to size (Appendix 3), or high speed (126 mph by A4 'Pacific' on LNE).

Within British restrictions, the virtues of three cylinders and four cylinders were about evenly matched. Four valves could be served by two valve gears and rocking levers. Three cylinders needed either three gears or two plus a 'conjugating' mechanism that needed more careful maintenance than sufficed for rocking levers.

Four cylinders with eight exhaust beats per revolution

required either four valve gears or a conjugated mechanism
that was nearly as complicated. The LMS 'Princesses' although
four-beat had four valve gears in order to avoid the imperfections in valve-drive through rocking levers.

Four cylinders compelled driving axleboxes to be narrower
than the greatest width possible with three cylinders, but if
the outside cylinders drove the wheels on the crank axle, the
horizontal loads on the axleboxes were low and so width
restriction was less important.

With axlebox width in mind, 20 ins was about the biggest
desirable diameter for inside cylinders. Station platform
clearance limited outside cylinders to 22 ins in diameter.
The greatest total volume of four equal cylinders was about
10 per cent more than for three equal cylinders. Four
cylinders need not all be equal but British design rarely took
advantage of this fact. For example, outside cylinders 22 ins ×
30 ins with two inside cylinders 20 ins × 26 ins have 30 per
cent greater volume than three 22 ins × 26 ins cylinders.

POSITIONS OF CYLINDERS

Three or four cylinders might be placed 'in line' over the
centre of the bogie, which in this scheme had to be sufficiently
far ahead of the leading coupled axle to leave room for a
connecting-rod between an inside crosshead and the cranked
leading axle. Fig 12A shows this layout and examples of it
were found in LNE classes B16 and D49 (R64 and R27) and
in the North Western 'Claughton' (R68). The valves might
be independently driven (B16) or the inside valve(s) might
derive their motion from the outside valves by mechanism
behind the valve chests (D49) or ahead of them ('Claughton').
The inside glands were reasonably accessible from under the
engine if there were no valve gear behind them ('Claughton'),
rather less so if the valves were driven from the rear (D49)
or awkward to reach if the space behind the cylinders was

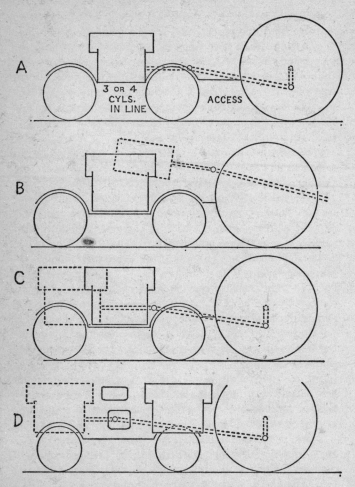

12. Positions of three cylinders or four cylinders
    A   LNW 'Claughton' 4/4-6-0 R68
    B   GN R116   LNE R118 R119
    C   LMS R59-62
    D   GW 4/4-6-0 R65-67   LMS 'Princess' R127

Within the figure:

A 3 OR 4 CYLS. IN LINE ACCESS

packed with mechanism (B16). In the easier cases, the space
between the leading coupled wheels and the preceding
wheels permitted a man to pass between them and to work
on the mechanism whilst standing on solid ground between
the rails. Where (as in many locomotives) the wheels were
too close together to admit a man in this way, he had to
work from a pit between the rails and to stand on a brake-
beam or whatever even less convenient foothold he could
find, to reach the valve-spindle glands.

Where the leading coupled axle was too close to the bogie
to permit an inside cylinder to be placed over its centre, the
cylinder might be set farther ahead, eg, LY 4-6-0 (R71 and
72) and 3/4-6-os (R59 to 62), or might be set high enough
for the inside connecting-rod to extend over the leading
coupled axle to drive a crank on the one behind it, eg,
Gresley 3/2-6-0 (R83) and 'Pacifics' (R116 to 118).

The former scheme (Fig 12C) placed the inside glands as
far out of reach as they could possibly be and would not have
been contemplated for one moment by any designer who
thought that he himself might ever have to 'service' such an
engine. Access to the inside glands meant climbing and
pushing into a very restricted space between the bottom of
the smokebox and the cross-member that carried the bogie-
pin.

In the alternative scheme (Fig 12B) access to the glands
was not difficult, provided that the drive to the inside valve
was by mechanism ahead of the valve chest as it was in
Gresley three-cylinder locomotives.

The Great Western and Great Southern & Western (Ireland) four-cylinder engines (R65, 66, 67, 74) and the LMS
'Princess' 'Pacifics' (R127) had inside cylinders abreast of
the leading bogie wheels and outside cylinders abreast of the
rear bogie wheels. The last feature was bad because the outside cylinders were attached to the frame where it was
weakened by being cut away to clear the bogie wheels, and
very substantial cross members had to be provided to

Duchess of Montrose taking the LMS 'Mid-day Scot' northward past
South Kenton

R1 Under buffer beam is pick-up for Automatic Warning Control

R2 Vacuum ejector near smokebox. Sniffing valve ahead of front splasher

R6 Long wheelbase. Small wheels

R8 Wartime economy. No running-board. No splashers

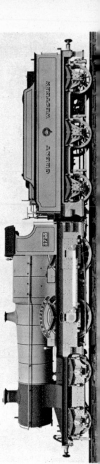

R9 One of the last batch of double-frame engines to be built

R12 Later tenders had 'solid' top rail

R26 The original 'Midland compound' modified by Deeley

R28 Finest 4-4-0 in Britain and probably in the world

R34 One of a number fitted with feed-water heater

R53 Beneath slide-bar is air-pump. Later replaced in favour of small ejector

R59 Bogie brakes, cylinder relief valves and air-pump, all later removed

R62 Double chimney. Top feed to boiler

R68 Walschaerts valve gear partly hidden by extended coupling-rod splasher

R67 Largest development of Churchward 'Star'. Plate-frame bogie

R76 Differs from 4300 class in having side-window cab and screw-reverse

R83 Early example (built 1924) of the Darlington version of the GN design

R87 Cast-iron wheel-centres. Three separate coupling-rods on each side

R94 With superheater. Header-discharge valve on smokebox

R99 Last Churchward design. First GW engine with outside steam pipes from smokebox

R102 Engines of this design were built by all four groups during World War II

R105 Original form. Chimney, safety valves, and rear bearings afterwards altered

R107 First GN 'Large Atlantic' restored to original condition after fifty years' service

R112 Air-pump for Westinghouse brake. 'Pop' safety valves

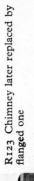

R129 Heaviest British ten-wheel locomotive. Noticeable departure from established practice of using outside steam pipes

R123 Chimney later replaced by flanged one

R114 Outside rods to work regulator in smokebox. Foot-plate extended over front of tender-frame

R124 BR rebuild of Bulleid 'Pacific'

R132 Second of P2 class (the first of the class was the only one to have poppet valves)

R128 In original form with single chimney. Boiler lagging cut away locally to clear lubricator lids when lifted

R133 Outside rods to work regulator in dome

R134 Used only for assisting trains up the I in 37 incline between Bromsgrove and Blackwell

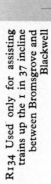

R208 Conical bunker rotatable to bring down coal

brace the outside cylinders and the frame into a rigid unit, whereas in other arrangements the inside cylinder-block performed this function. Moreover, the need to clear the rear bogie wheels when laterally displaced from their central position limited cylinder diameters to a maximum of about 16 ins.

But by cutting away the frame-plates above the bogie centre, quite good access was provided to the inside glands (Fig 12D). On the other hand, much of the inside valve gear was very hard to reach; by having no inside valve gear, the Great Southern & Western engines (R74) made the very most of this cylinder layout.

GENERAL

It may be suggested that the main advantage of using more than two cylinders was the possibility of attaining a high nominal tractive effort without high boiler pressure, but there were designs, eg, LMS 3/4-6-os (R59 to 62) and the one BR three-cylinder locomotive (class 8 'Pacific'), in which no advantage was taken of this. For high power at high speed the use of more than two cylinders might be justified by reduced hammer-blow on the track and reduced vibration in the engine itself.

FOUR-CYLINDER LOCOMOTIVES

The most numerous group of four-cylinder locomotives in Great Britain in the first decade of the twentieth century had a special justification for that feature. They were compound (ie, double expansion) engines of the London & North Western Railway and compounding demands more than two cylinders if the engine is not to be unsymmetrical. The North Western had built a great many three-cylinder compound engines with in-built defects and had turned to four-cylinder compounds as offering better prospects. Here, again, the cylinders were not of common diameter, as double expansion means greater volume of steam in the second stage than in the first and so the total volume of the low-pressure cylinders must be greater than that of the high-pressure cylinders.

In general a locomotive that was to use steam from the boiler in each of four cylinders was given a common diameter and a common piston stroke for all four cylinders. In some designs the outside cylinders drove the wheels on the crank axle which was usually the leading coupled axle. Where restriction of wheelbase would have brought the outside cylinders so close to the leading coupled axle as to have made the connecting-rods unacceptably short, the outside cylinders drove the second pair of coupled wheels. This 'divided drive' was sometimes claimed to be superior to the 'single-axle' drive, whereas the latter gave smoother running because its balancing forces were not transmitted through the axleboxes. The bending moments in the crank axle were bigger, but this did no harm if the axles were properly designed to withstand them.

Among the British locomotives that had four cylinders with no commending distinction may be mentioned the London & South Western 4/4-6-0 No 330 built in 1905 to the designs of D. Drummond. It was for a time 'the largest locomotive in Great Britain' and it was certainly one of the worst. The outside cylinders were set on the frame in a position where they overlapped the rims of the leading coupled wheels and the attachment bolts were located in a length only about half that of the cylinder-casting; as an inevitable consequence the outside cylinders continually worked loose.

The outside steam chests were underneath the cylinders, right down at rail level, about as far from the boiler and the blast-pipe as they could be. Parts of the Walschaerts valve gear were only a few inches above rail level. The grate was long, high, and almost parallel to the rails so that firing was very laborious.

These locomotives were unsuccessful and variants with smaller boilers were no better. Later on a generally similar design was developed with four cylinders in the normal position under the smokebox and with 6 ft 7 ins driving wheels. These engines (the 443 class) were tolerable, although unfair on firemen, but their work did not surpass that of the best South Western 4-4-0s, the 463 class introduced in 1912.

It was the smooth running of French-built four-cylinder compound 'Atlantics' that inspired the Great Western to try a four-cylinder simple 'Atlantic' of the same general size and form. This was No 40 *North Star* built in 1906, and characterized by having the two inside cylinders abreast of the leading bogie wheels and the other two abreast of the rear bogie wheels. In the latter vicinity the frame-plates were tied by a substantial cross-stay that supported the expansion links of what was virtually Walschaerts valve gear applied to the inside valves. Rocking levers behind the inside cylinders and ahead of the outside cylinders applied the appropriate motions to the outside valves.

Each expansion link was oscillated by a connexion to the crosshead on the adjacent cylinder line and no eccentric was necessary. This was no new idea but, nevertheless, R. M. Deeley of the Midland Railway had obtained a patent on something like it, and the Great Western never used it again.

Openings in the frame-plates above the bogie centre made inside glands, crossheads, and much of the valve gear reasonably accessible from outside the frame. This facility was provided after No 40 had been in service for some time.

North Star was found to be quite a good engine but it was quickly decided that she would have been better as a 4-6-0 and was so converted in 1912. By that time, however, some forty similar 4-6-0s (the 'Stars') had been built and their work had already gone a long way towards establishing the Great Western four-cylinder 4-6-0 as one of the major triumphs in British locomotive history. In power-for-size, speed, and economy of fuel they set standards that were unequalled for about twenty years and barely surpassed at all.

The Churchward example probably inspired the Lancashire & Yorkshire Railway to go in for four-cylinder 4-6-os and Horwich works produced the first of a class of twenty in 1908. These engines were conventional in design and impressively large in appearance. The outside cylinders were abreast of the bogie centre and slightly behind the inside cylinders whose piston-rod glands and valve-spindle glands were therefore lamentably difficult to reach for servicing. Joy valve gear applied to the inside connecting-rods drove the inside valves directly and the outside valves by rocking levers. Balanced flat valves were used for all four cylinders.

Alterations were made to chimney, petticoat-pipe, blastpipe, and ashpan after disappointing early trials, but the engines were still sluggish and could not be relied upon to beat the 7 ft 3 ins 'Atlantics' in handling the most difficult LY passenger-train duties even over the steepest gradients. The 'Dreadnoughts' (as these four-cylinder engines were sometimes called) were hard to keep in running order and E. Mason recalls (Bib. 8) a time when all twenty were under repair at once. They had imperfections in smokebox, valves, and ashpan and LY enginemen generally regarded them as 'failures'. Certainly they were considerably improved by rebuilding (from 1921) with superheaters, piston valves and Walschaerts valve gear and, after the LY had become amalgamated with the LNW in 1922, the Horwich engines were tried on the main line from Crewe to Carlisle. Early results encouraged the Horwich authorities (who obtained precedence over those at Crewe after their common absorption into the LMS in 1923) to build slightly enlarged Horwich 4-6-os for the Euston–Carlisle route but in regular service even these failed to equal the performance of the North Western engines and so did not supersede them.

For its express passenger trains between London and Liverpool, Manchester and Carlisle, the North Western built 130 four-cylinder 'Claughton' class 4-6-os between 1913 and 1923 and these engines, together with North Western 'Georges' and 'Princes', continued to run those trains till near the end of 1927.

In some ways the 'Claughton' design (R68) was superior to that of the Great Western four-cylinder engines, for example in accessibility of the main mechanism, but imperfections in detail made the 'Claughtons' inferior over prolonged periods in service. For example, oil-feed to the rear-axle bearings was to their tops (the worst place), and was through pipes in such positions that, when things became worn, the rims of the wheels could cut through the pipes, and bearings without oil soon ran into trouble.

It is almost incredible that a defect of this sort could be built into a locomotive that was to be the pride of the 'Premier Line' in Great Britain but alas! such things did happen on many railways; moreover, many of the errors were never corrected and locomotive men had to live their lives under wholly unnecessary handicaps. The 'Claughton' design included an ashpan that restricted air-flow to the grate, a blast-pipe-and-chimney layout that was far from ideal, and valves that did not long remain steam-tight. But they were magnificent-looking engines in a Victorian style, dwarfing their co-workers on the North Western and forbidding any observer to imagine that they had any defect; in fact, they could have been made into very much better engines without altering their appearance at all. If that had been done, the 'Claughtons' might have produced the performance of the Great Western 'Castles' ten years before the first 'Castle' was built.

In 1917 the Great Central built a four-cylinder 4-6-0 1169 *Lord Faringdon* (R69) comparable in size with the 'Claughtons,' but with outside cylinders driving the middle pair of coupled wheels and with Stephenson valve gear driving the inside valves by rocking levers on spindles extended through the frame-plates (behind the cylinders) to carry arms that worked the outside valves. It was a four-cylinder equivalent of the 'Sir Sam Fay' class of 4-6-0 which had two large inside cylinders, correspondingly narrow axleboxes and correspondingly high bearing pressures associated with horizontal forces. *Lord Faringdon* may have been conceived as a means of getting better axlebox performance than could be expected of the 'Sir Sams' if worked really hard. *Lord Faringdon* (and five sisters built before 1923) had, however, defects similar to those of the 'Claughtons' and their performance on the principal Great Central passenger trains was much less satisfactory than that of the 'Director' class 4-4-0s.

Locomotives (R70) generally similar to the 'Faringdons' but with 5 ft 8 ins wheels were built as mixed-traffic locomotives to a total of thirty-eight. Enginemen unofficially reported them to be very heavy on coal and there has been no officially published information to refute this criticism.

On the whole, therefore, four-cylinder locomotives did not distinguish themselves favourably in British locomotive history but this was because they had defects not peculiarly associated with the number of cylinders. On the other hand, the four-cylinder engines built by the Great Western Railway were for about twenty years the best British locomotives for heavy, fast passenger trains. The 'Stars' (R65) had been given four cylinders rather than two because of the much better balance of the reciprocating parts, even though it made them expensive alternatives to two-cylinder engines (the 'Saints') of the same wheel arrangement (4-6-0) with the same design of boiler (the Swindon No 1 standard). Between 1903 and 1923, the Great Western built some 73 locomotives of the four-cylinder 'Star' class and 76 'Saints'. During that period the most difficult express passenger-train duties were normally given to the 'Stars', which were amply numerous to cover them, and so it was impossible for any unofficial observer (and difficult for anyone) to discover whether

either class had any overall advantage over the other in
regularly doing the hardest Great Western work.

Great Western opinion on the subject of four cylinders
versus two may be judged from the fact that, in the twenty-
five years between the grouping of British railways in 1923
and nationalization of them in 1948, the Swindon Works
built about 170 slightly enlarged 'Stars' (the 'Castles'), 30
'Kings' (enlarged 'Castles'), 330 two-cylinder 'Saints' with
driving wheels reduced in diameter by 8 ins (the 'Halls')
and 80 others with driving wheels 4 ins smaller still (the
'Granges').

Stanier applied Great Western four-cylinder technique to
twelve 'Pacifics' built by the LMS from 1933, but subsequent
LMS 'Pacifics' had four cylinders arranged differently. This
suggested that experience with the earlier engines convinced
the LMS design staff that something better could be done.

The culmination of pre-nationalization British locomotive
development in the LMS 'Duchess' was a triumph for the
four-cylinder principle, first successfully demonstrated in
Britain by Great Western practice. One doubt may, however,
be expressed. Dynamometer car tests (Bib. 9) on a Great
Western 'King' showed internal resistance to be dissipating
a much greater fraction of its cylinder power than was common in two-cylinder engines. Was the smooth running of
four-cylinder engines too dearly bought?

Early in 1920 the Midland produced the famous 'Lickey
banker' No 2290 (R134) for assisting trains up the two miles
at 1 in 37 between Bromsgrove and Blackwell on the Birmingham–Bristol main line. (In travelling on this incline one may
detect the slope without looking outside the compartment.)

It was a 0-10-0, with two outside cylinders driving the
middle pair of wheels and two inside cylinders driving the
middle axle; the second axle was also cranked to clear the inside connecting-rods. The valves, worked by Walschaerts
gear, were above, and slightly farther apart than the outside
cylinders. Each valve-head controlled steam for the adjacent

outside cylinder-end and also for the opposite end of the adjacent inside cylinder through a port nearly 3 ft long. This was not so disadvantageous as to prevent the engine from 'banking' for nearly forty years, but no similar one was built. It had steam-operated brakes in accordance with current Midland practice, but it was probably the only tender engine in England to have a hand-brake in 1920.

The 1 in 7 inclination of the cylinders of No 2290 was in sharp contrast to the zero slope in Britain's only other 0-10-0 the Great Eastern 'Decapod' tank engine (R207), where the designer's fear of any inclination at all led him to use an inside connecting rod in the form of an A-frame surrounding the leading axle.

Only two designs of four-cylinder tank engine worked in Great Britain. The first of them was a 0-6-0 tank engine built by the North Stafford Railway in 1922. The reason for using four cylinders seems to have been a desire to obtain a more nearly uniform tractive effort than is possible with any smaller number of cylinders, this being achieved by setting the cranks so that the engine gave eight beats per revolution of the driving wheels. This was the first time this had been done in Great Britain. The cylinders were inclined to the rails at 1 in 9 and the outside ones well overlapped the leading coupled wheels, and so their attachment to the frame plates was probably as insecure as that of the similarly placed cylinders on the early South Western 4-6-0s. Each valve was worked by its own set of Walschaerts gear.

The locomotive was thus made a good deal more complicated than the ordinary 0-6-0T, in order to extract about 8 per cent more tractive effort from the adhesion weight which was nearly 57 tons. On the other hand, sand-pipes were applied only to the front and back of the middle pair of wheels, leaving about one-third of the total weight ineffective on slippery rails.

The engine was later stripped of tanks and bunker and attached to a tender to become the only four-cylinder 0-6-0 in

British history. There is no published information about the
performance of this engine in either form.

The LY authorities were so pleased with the rebuilt Horwich four-cylinder 4-6-0s that they stretched the design by
lengthening the frame to carry a bunker over a rear bogie
and by lengthening the leading bogie and the firebox. Side-
tanks were added but weight restriction compelled them to
be short. Even so, at almost 100 tons, these were the heaviest
British locomotives when built in 1924. At that they were some
19 tons lighter than the Horwich 4-6-0 plus tender and the
intention behind them may have been to use them instead of
tender engines for the principal trains on the LY system
which was well provided with water-troughs. There is,
however, no published record of their performance in fast
service and much of the work given to them could be done
more economically by the much smaller 2-4-2 tank engines of
the LY.

The failure of the first batch of Horwich 4-6-4 tank engines
to justify themselves was realized early enough for frame-
plates prepared for later ones to be shortened and used for
4-6-0s. With the possible exception of the LBS class of
seven, British 4-6-4 tank engines were never conspicuously
successful and the limited career of the Horwich examples
suggests that they were less so than any others.

Although a four-cylinder engine was a more 'refined'
machine than a two-cylinder one of the same power, in
running more smoothly and in inflicting less punishment on
the track, it was an expensive luxury. This was immediately
obvious to enginemen because of the greater quantities of
oil they had to carry from the stores and of the time they had
to spend under the boiler in attending to the mechanism
between the frame-plates. These matters were not specially
important to those in authority in the years before World
War I, but rising costs gradually altered the picture and,
when new standard designs of locomotive were being considered for British Railways after nationalization in 1948, an

early decision was to produce only two-cylinder locomotives
and no crank axle.

THREE-CYLINDER LOCOMOTIVES

Three-cylinder engines had occasionally been tried on
British railways during the nineteenth century but they did
not start to become numerous until well into the twentieth.
Curiously, but quite insignificantly, the layout was favoured
more in the eastern half of Britain than in the west. The
Great Eastern's giant ten-wheel well-tank engine was the
first embodiment of it after 1900, and there it was employed
for the good reason that there was insufficient room for two
cylinders large enough to develop the required tractive
effort without going up to a higher boiler pressure than most
designers liked at the time. This locomotive was built
purely to demonstrate that a steam locomotive could acceler-
ate a 300-ton train from rest to a speed of 30 mph in 30
seconds on level track. This it did after modifications that
must have included raising its boiler pressure from the
originally quoted 200 psi to somewhere about 250; 200
would just have sufficed if there had been no windage or
sliding surfaces.

The next three examples of three-cylinder locomotives
were also tank engines, the Great Central building four
3/0-8-4Ts for hump-pushing at Wath in 1908, the North
Eastern building four 3/4-8-0Ts also for hump-pushing and
twenty 3/4-6-2Ts for short-distance goods trains.

Sir Vincent Raven had by then (1910) become enthusiastic
about three-cylinder engines and in 1911 produced the first
of the class Z three-cylinder 'Atlantics' (R112) eventually to
number fifty. In 1913 came the first of the class D 3/4-4-4Ts
(R180) and after World War I came ten 3/4-6-0s (class S3
on the North Eastern, class B16 on the LNE) and ten 3/0-8-0s
(R97) (class T3 on the North Eastern, class Q7 on the LNE).

Finally the North Eastern managed to complete the first of five three-cylinder 'Pacifics' just before the railways were grouped at the beginning of 1923.

All these Vincent Raven classes were identical in that the three cylinders were set in line abreast over the centre of the bogie and the pistons pulled and pushed cranks in the leading coupled wheels and in their axle. Two sets of Stephenson valve gear worked piston valves alongside the outside cylinders, and a third set worked through an offsetting arm a piston valve above the middle cylinder. Packing four eccentrics between an axlebox and a crank web was not easy; it led to a weak crank axle in the North Eastern 'Pacific'.

Possibly inspired by this fashion at Darlington, Gresley built a 3/2-8-o at Doncaster in 1918. In major dimensions it was similar to 2/2-8-os (R100) introduced in 1913; in these engines the connecting-rods were on crankpins in the third pair of coupled wheels. In the three-cylinder engines (R104), however, the crankpins were in the second pair of coupled wheels and their axle. Gresley concentrated the drive on one axle in all his subsequent three-cylinder designs except the 'Sandringham' 3/4-6-os (R63) (LNE class B17) of which the first was built by the North British Locomotive Company in 1928.

In the original 3/2-8-o (No 461), outside Walschaerts valve gear drove two rocking shafts from which hanging arms took the drive to piston valves above the outside cylinders but not so widely separated as these cylinders. The valve for the inside cylinder was alongside it on the left of the locomotive's centreline, and received its motion from a linkage connected to both rocking shafts. Kinematically (which means everything assumed to be perfectly rigid and weightless with no slackness in any joint) the mechanism was almost perfect, but to most practical engineers it did not 'look right' and it was never repeated. When Gresley realized that something better was needed he consulted Mr H. Holcroft who had made a basic study of all such 'conjugated mechanisms' (David Joy had used one many years earlier on triple-expansion marine engines), and between them they evolved the much more satisfactory scheme (Fig 5B, p 13) that was applied in the course of time to hundreds of LNE three-cylinder locomotives and was commonly associated with the name of Gresley (Bib. 38, 39). Its first use was in Gresley's first 3/2-6-0, No 1000 (R83) of the Great Northern Railway, built in 1920. This locomotive was also distinctive in that the diameter (6 ft) of its boiler barrel at the *front* end was exceeded in only one other British locomotive, Gresley's 'Garratt' 2-8-8-2 of 1925.

Although the conjugated mechanism was kinematically very simple it introduced some new problems in valve setting and some of the first ten 3/2-6-0s had comically uneven exhaust beats when first turned out.

Later on there was bother of a different nature in that un-pleasant noises came from the inside valve when the engine was drifting fast with the reversing gear set to give the valves their maximum travel as was common practice. Examination showed that the actual maximum travel was greater than pure kinematics suggested. It was then realized that steel is heavy but not rigid and that slackness developed in pin joints. This defect was eventually removed by re-design with stronger mechanism and eliminating slackness at certain joints by using roller bearings but the 'scare' persisted and had an extraordinarily regrettable consequence.

The diameter (8 ins) and lap ($1\frac{1}{2}$ ins) of the valves used in the 3/2-6-0s were about right for the cylinder volume and for the moderate speeds of the fast goods trains for which the class was intended. What happened later suggests that this was more by accident than by design. For in the first Gresley 'Pacifics' the same valve diameter of 8 ins was used with 20-in cylinders and, in order to avoid risk of damage by over-running of the inside valve, the maximum valve-travel was reduced by cutting the lap down to 1·25 ins and the latest cut-off to 65 per cent instead of the usual 75 or more. This gave the Great Western the victory in the 1925 'locomotive exchange'.

First sight of the underside of the Gresley 'Pacific' made enginemen think that something was missing. There was certainly no valve gear, no eccentric and no reversing gear; just one piston rod, crosshead, connecting-rod, and crank. There was not much to be looked after and there was plenty of space round it. This was the result of driving the inside valve by mechanism lying under hinged plates on the running-board ahead of the smokebox. This mechanism received its motion from forward extensions of the outside valve-spindles through mechanism similar to that used in the 3/2-6-0s. The Gresley 'Pacific' was a very good engine right from the start, but it was not excellent. This was because its valves were not big enough to handle the full boiler output of steam at an economical cut-off. The 'Pacifics' roared along like outsize Ivatt 'Atlantics' and the firemen fought to keep them fed. After 1925, Gresley 'Pacifics' were given better valves and valve gear, and their coal consumption came down very markedly, but even better could have been done without pressing the boilers beyond 180 psi.

By careful test Gresley established that 220 psi instead of 180 did not significantly increase the coal consumption per unit of work done (Bib. 12). He accepted the heavier boiler and higher boiler maintenance cost that high pressure demanded and found that the 220 psi A3 'Pacific' was a little faster than the original A1, because the cylinders were smaller in relation to the valves (R116, 118, 119). In the A4, a boiler pressure of 250 psi enabled 18½-in cylinders to be used with 9-in valves and this enabled the engine to get up to 110 mph or so down the ten-mile Essendine bank. With a double chimney and a remorseless driver, 126 mph was reached in 1938. This last was merely gallery play. The real value of the Gresley 'Pacific' was ability to average 75 mph over long distances with 330-ton trains or 60 mph with 650-ton trains.

CHAPTER FIVE

MORE THAN TEN WHEELS

THE OBVIOUS wheel arrangement for a fast and powerful twelve-wheel locomotive was 4-6-2.

The 'Atlantic' (4-4-2) had room for a big wide firebox but only about half the total weight could be placed on the coupled wheels.

The 4-6-0 gripped the rails well but the grate area could not exceed about 34 sq ft without extending the firebox to a point where even a sloping grate was hard to fire.

The 4-6-2 ('Pacific') offered a way out of both difficulties. It permitted the use of a wide firebox and about 50 per cent more adhesion weight than could be allowed on four wheels. The carrying wheels under the firebox prevented the backward pull of the drawbar from laying more weight on the coupled wheels, as it did in 4-6-0s, and so a 4-6-2 would be more likely to slip than a 4-6-0 with the same nominal adhesion weight, but the enginemen would learn how to cope with this. (It was not easy where uneven track caused the trailing wheels to take most of the weight.)

The first standard-gauge 'Pacific' to run in Great Britain was the Great Western *The Great Bear* built in 1908. There was no need then, or ever afterwards, for a Great Western locomotive of that size and no one knows for certain why it was built. The cylinders and the first ten wheels were virtually identical with those of the 'Star' class 4-6-0s. To decide what to do about the boiler and the rear truck was more difficult as there were not many proved 'Pacifics' in the whole world at that time. So Churchward had to do more guessing than usual; the engine never equalled the best efforts of the 'Stars'

(R65), very rarely left the Paddington–Bristol main line, and ran half its mileage on goods trains. The Great Western kept quiet about it, Churchward expressed a willingness to sell it, and, when its boiler had got past economical repair, the rest of the engine was cut down to form the basis of a 'Castle'.

The next British 'Pacific' was built by the Great Northern in 1922. There was no mistake about the boiler. The firebox had a forward extension to give adequate furnace volume (*The Great Bear* was defective here); the boiler barrel was 6 ft 5 ins in diameter at the firebox end and tapered to 5 ft 6 ins at the smokebox. Cylinders and valves were laid out as in the three-cylinder 2-6-os, introduced by Gresley in 1920, but valves of only 8-in diameter and 1·25-in lap were provided for cylinders 20 ins by 26 ins and this had a lamentable consequence not only for Gresley 'Pacifics' but for British steam locomotive practice in general.

These valves were not large enough in relation to the cylinders to produce performance of Swindon quality, but it was not till after the defeat of Gresley 'Pacifics' by Great Western 'Castles' in the 1925 locomotive exchange that Gresley became convinced of this. Increase in valve lap by less than half an inch transformed the A1 'Pacifics'. Moves in the same direction in later designs produced LNE 'Pacifics' that could be criticized only for their unnecessarily high boiler pressures.

With 'grouping' of the railways impending, the North Eastern decided that prestige demanded a 'Pacific' and so it hurriedly produced one (R117) that was simply an enlarged and extended class Z 'Atlantic' (R112) hardly more effective than the similarly conceived *Great Bear*.

The LMS produced no 'Pacific' till 1933 when Stanier's first design (R127) was seen to be a *Great Bear* with an enlarged and improved firebox, with the cylinders, motion, and boiler pressure of the Great Western 'King' and with a 'gimmick' in the form of a separate set of valve gear for

each of the four cylinders; its early performance was unim-
pressive. Boilers with greater firebox volume were provided
for LMS 'Princesses' after the first two, and in a year or
two they were out-performing the 'Royal Scots'.

Different detail modifications made to most of the twelve
'Princesses' showed that not everyone on the LMS approved
of them and, in 1937, a better design (R128) was produced
but largely concealed by a streamlined casing.

The first Southern 'Pacifics' (R124) were designed and
built during World War II and appeared in 1941. The object
seems to have been to have a tested-and-proved 'Pacific'
design to build after the war. These engines had a number of
unconventional features that were well worth trying. That
some of them were not worth keeping became clear to
everyone but the chief mechanical engineer who was, moreover, able to persuade the management to build over a
hundred slightly freakish 'Pacifics', a great many of which
were afterwards rebuilt by British Railways into conventional
locomotives.

Some at least of the streamline casings of Southern 'Pacifics' were made of not-wholly-metallic material of which no
details were published.

In 1925 the LNE built two 3/2-8-2s (R131) with boilers
identical with those of the current Gresley 'Pacifics'. They
were intended for taking heavy goods trains on the main
line between London and Doncaster and could do so admir-
ably. Unfortunately, trains long enough to make the use of
these big engines economic were too long for many of the
'lay-by' sidings in which goods trains had to take refuge from
the fast passenger trains on that route. As this was known
before the engines were designed, they can have been built
only in the hope that once they had shown what they could do,
the management might be persuaded to lengthen the sidings.
This did not happen and the P1 class never numbered more
than two.

In 1932–3 Gresley had been impressed (as were many other

people) by the exploits of Chapelon 4C/4-8-0s on the steeply graded Paris–Orleans route between Vierzon and Toulouse. The LNE route from Edinburgh to Aberdeen had steep gradients, numerous speed restrictions and some heavy trains, and so it offered scope for a British equivalent of the Chapelon 4-8-0. But Gresley was a firm 'wide fire-box man' and so he produced, instead of 3/4-8-0s, a large 3/2-8-2 (R132) that was strained by the sharper curves because the outside slide-bars precluded the spring-controlled side-play that might otherwise have been provided in the leading coupled axle. The first engine resembled the Chapelon engines in having Kylchap double blast-pipes, poppet valves, and feed-water heater.

On test the first P2 took 650 tons from King's Cross to Grantham at an average speed of 56 mph but this was no better than Gresley 'Pacifics' could do.

Coal consumption in service was unofficially reported to be very high and later engines were built with piston valves and Walschaerts valve gear.

The practice of changing engines at Dundee limited engine trips to about 80 miles. This specially disfavoured the use of large locomotives and the 3/2-8-2s built for this service were not conspicuously successful in it. On straight routes with longer non-stop runs they might have given more value for money, although even then unlikely to beat Gresley 'Pacifics'. After Gresley's death, Thompson had the 3/2-8-2s rebuilt as 'Pacifics' markedly unlike Gresley 'Pacifics' and markedly less able to cope with the difficulties of the Aberdeen line.

Among British tender engines the only twelve-wheelers apart from 'Pacifics' and 2-8-2s were 2/2-10-0s. The first design of this wheel arrangement was an enlargement of the wartime 'Austerity' 2/2-8-0s. They were built for post-occupation use in Europe and not much was seen of them in Britain. The only other British 2-10-0s (R133) were those of British Railways class 9 and these are discussed on pp 152–5.

CHAPTER SIX

POST-GROUPING CHANGES

CHANGE ON THE LMS

FOR THE first eight or nine years of the existence of the LMS group, the writhing tangle of its higher management so bedevilled the possibilities of locomotive development that even the slow progress that was made was a miracle.

After the death of C. J. Bowen-Cooke, in 1920, control of North Western locomotive matters passed to H. P. M. Beames at a time when the need was for post-war rehabilitation rather than for new developments. At the beginning of 1922 the North Western became amalgamated with the much smaller Lancashire & Yorkshire Railway whose general manager was, however, promoted to the corresponding position in the enlarged North Western Railway and whose locomotive superintendent, G. Hughes, was given charge of motive power of the huge LMS group, which in 1923 combined the enlarged North Western, the Midland, the Caledonian, the Glasgow & South Western, the Highland, and some minor railways.

So a locomotive department that had to cope with hard running over long distances on the West Coast main line came under the charge of an engineer whose recent care was of locomotives working comfortably over only short distances.

When Hughes retired in 1925 his place was taken by Sir Henry Fowler, who had been the head of the Midland Railway locomotive department. He was not so much a locomotive engineer as a workshop production manager and an organizer of large-scale manufacture during World War I. This work had earned him his knighthood.

So the locomotive department that still had to cope with hard running over long distances then came under the control of officials of a railway on which it was forbidden to try to get hard work out of any locomotive. On the Midland there were plenty of spare locomotives at hand to 'double-head' any train that was not light and there were officials everywhere to see that double-heading took place. To Midland men, the Smith-Johnson-Deeley-Fowler 3/4-4-0 compound engine (R26) was the consummation devoutly to be worshipped. Locomotive matters on the LMS were in a mess and it did not need the flooding of the West Coast main lines with newly built Midland compounds to demonstrate the fact.

As a proposal for locomotives to handle the West Coast mainline trains, Midland staff produced a design for a 'Pacific' that was to be a compound because the biggest Midland engine was a compound and no Midland man could imagine any big engine that was *not* a compound. On the other hand, North Western men, with bitter experience never to be forgotten, declined to consider any new design that *was* a compound. North Western engines tended to be condemned for glaring faults in vital details, and for high cost in coal and maintenance, but no others in the whole LMS could take the West Coast main-line trains single-handed.

In the meantime there had been tremendous publicity in 1925 for the locomotive exchanges between the Great Western and the LNE, in which the claim of the former to possess in the 'Castle' 'the most powerful passenger engine' in Great Britain was superficially vindicated. In 1926 the Southern announced that its new *Lord Nelson* (R75) had won this distinction because its nominal tractive effort was higher than that of the 'Castle'.

It was clear that the LMS had to make some sort of entrance into this field of publicity. It was decided that the main day-train between London and Glasgow should be

raised in status and glamorized in 1927 and that as part of
the uplift a new design of locomotive was needed. There
was also a technical need for something superior to anything
the LMS then had. That a Great Western 'Castle' could fill
this bill was obvious from published information and so it
was proposed that, as the 'Castle' was a well-proved design,
some should be built for the LMS. The LMS technical men
sought to kill this bright scheme by pointing out that the
'Castle' was several inches too wide to be a standard locomotive on the LMS.

This the operating division countered by running a Great
Western 'Castle' on the hardest West Coast main-line
trains between Euston and Carlisle for a fortnight; without
fuss it did the work punctually and economically. This was
in October/November 1926 and, as the new train (to be
called *The Royal Scot*) was to begin running in 1927, the new
locomotive design had to get moving. The management had
evidently no confidence that the LMS technical staff could
do this without help and so it was arranged for a Midland
man to discuss with opposite numbers of the Southern the
possibility of using the *Lord Nelson* design for the LMS.
Smarting under the suggestion that they could not do their
job, the LMS staff evidently resolved that the outcome of the
move should at least not *look* like any predecessor and right
well they succeeded in this. The final compromise, the
'Royal Scot' (R59), was a stubbed and uglified version of the
virtually untried 'Lord Nelson', but with only one inside
cylinder tucked as far out of reach as possible under the front
of the smokebox. It was known that the Great Western were
adopting 250-psi boiler pressure in a new design to beat the
'Nelson's' nominal tractive effort and, although the LMS
had probably agreed not to do this, they decided not to be
beaten by the Great Western on boiler pressure. So the new
4-6-0 had 250 psi with no technical justification, as must
have been known at the time and as was demonstrated three
or four years later when the slightly smaller 'Baby Scots'

(R60) with 200-psi boiler pressure showed that they could equal the 'Big Scots' in power, beat them in coal economy, in general repair cost (Bib. 10), and in boiler maintenance (Bib. 11). An ungainly wrapper-type smokebox of prodigious diameter flaunted rejection of Great Western practice in that component. A wind deflector (*capuchon*) 1 in high on a 7-in high chimney was merely a derisive comment on *capuchons* in general. An order placed with the North British Locomotive Co for fifty 3/4-6-0s of this untried design showed confidence if nothing else.

Adoption of the general layout of a three-cylinder compound 4-6-0 projected by Derby in 1924 would have provided far better access to the inside mechanism and, with strong side-control for the bogie and thin flanges (or none) on the leading coupled wheels, might have made a better-riding engine than the 'Scots' turned out to be.

The first 'Royal Scot' 3/4-6-0 went into service in the summer of 1927. It was adequate for its initial prestige job and for all others on the West Coast main line. After experience with them, some enginemen would occasionally extract notable feats in power and speed from newly repaired 'Royal Scots' but five or six years' running exposed weaknesses in design and it was quite clear that Great Western standards had not been attained. Wrapper-type smokebox, leaky valves, and indifferent axleboxes were defects that should never have been permitted in any design completed in 1927.

A 'Royal Scot' won temporary fame by achieving, on a dynamometer-car test, a figure of 2·66 lb of coal per drawbar-horsepower hour, surpassing the existing British record of 2·83 lb established by a 'Castle' in 1924. But alas! the LMS dynamometer was afterwards found to be behaving quite unreliably and so the figure of 2·66 had to be rejected. The true value was found to be about 3·3, in line with what had been recorded with re-boilered 'Claughtons' and Horwich 2-6-0s.

The 'Scots' soon showed that, when in good condition, they could do all that had been expected of them, but it was not until LMS 'Pacifics' appeared six years later that they gave of their best. This was partly due to the stimulus that a bigger engine always gave to drivers who had become used to the previous best and partly due to detail improvements (eg, less leaky valves) made to the 'Scots' after Stanier had come from the Great Western to put the LMS locomotive department in order.

The 'Scots' were so much better than any other main-line locomotives on the LMS that the three-cylinder principle was accepted with enthusiasm. Fifty-two similar but not quite so big locomotives (R60) were built, with boiler pressure 200 psi instead of 250 and general observation suggested that they were rather faster engines than the 'Scots'. They certainly livened matters up not only on the West Coast route but also on the Midland and GS route from London to Glasgow. These 'Baby Scots', or 'Patriots' as they were sometimes called later on, were taken as the basis of the Stanier 3/4-6-0 'Jubilees' (R61) introduced in 1935. These were superior to the 'Scots' and 'Baby Scots' in having cylindrical smokeboxes, improved axleboxes and in the advantageous details of their Swindon-style boilers. They were comparable in basic dimensions and ability with the Great Western 'Castles', and 190 of them were built.

Stanier's policy on the LMS was simply to apply Great Western methods to the useful limit in designing locomotives to meet current and foreseeable requirements. It was his easiest safe course and he had probably been instructed to adopt it anyway. It yielded good results (apart from one or two 'false starts' in certain details) and set up on the LMS standards by which any later development might be assessed. It underlay the development of LMS motive power to a level unsurpassed by any other group.

Stanier's first gesture was to produce a design for an LMS 'Pacific'; this materialized in the summer of 1933 and was later named *The Princess Royal*. Smokebox and cylinder layout was very similar to that of the Great Western 'King' except that each valve was driven by its own set of Walschaerts valve gear. The Belpaire-style wide firebox had only a suspicion of a combustion chamber and so it almost repeated a defect of Churchward's *The Great Bear*. This was corrected in the third and nine subsequent LMS 'Princesses' and these engines showed themselves to be capable of doing all that was required in running West Coast mainline trains.

The main defects in the first two 'Princesses' were that the firebox volume was rather small in relation to the grate area and that the use of a small superheater kept down the number of flues to the extent that the total cross-sectional area of the passage of hot gas through the boiler barrel was rather low. Boilers for the last ten 'Princesses' were better than the first two in these respects.

The cylinder layout of the 'Princess' was exactly that of Great Western practice except that, in order to provide adequate clearance of station platforms, the outside cylinders were set at a small angle to the plane of the rails whereas the inside cylinders were parallel to that plane. Each valve-spindle was parallel to the axis of the cylinder fed by the valve and so neither outside valve-spindle was parallel to the adjacent inside valve-spindle. This was unimportant as, in a surprising departure from common practice for four-beat four-cylinder engines, each valve had its own set of Walschaerts gear. Not everyone in authority agreed that this complication was useful, and one of the twelve 'Princesses' was later altered so that each outside valve gear worked the adjacent inside valve by means of a rocking lever and a connecting link specially arranged to accommodate the angle between the directions of motion of the valve-spindles.

In the 'Princesses' were incorporated many Great Western details such as closure of oil-boxes by corks that kept oil in and dirt out, but, by their porosity, prohibited air-lock. This feature of *Princess Elizabeth* caused some locomotivemen to call her 'Corky Liz'.

The publicity won by the streamline trains on the LNE compelled the LMS to follow suit and so a streamlined 'Pacific' was required. The opportunity was taken to design a larger 'Pacific' than the 'Princess', to get away from the restrictive setting of her outside cylinders and to avoid inside valve gear. No one expected accessibility in a streamlined locomotive and few LMS designers liked outside cylinders over bogie wheels. So the outside cylinders were placed between the bogie wheels and an opening in the frame-plate just ahead of each outside cylinder would at least have enabled the inside glands to be seen in strong sunlight after part of the streamlining casing had been removed. With the outside cylinders clear of the bogie wheels there was plenty of room for the larger diameter that would have permitted weight and money to be saved by building the boiler for 180-psi working pressure instead of 250. But prestige demanded equality with Swindon and Doncaster, whatever the cost, and so 250 was used. Ten locomotives of this oddly named 'Princess–Coronation' class were built and very comfortably ran the 330-ton 'Coronation Scot' train between London and Glasgow in 6½ hours with a change of enginemen at Carlisle.

Five essentially identical locomotives (R128) without streamlining were built later and these 'Duchesses' were perhaps the most majestic-looking locomotives ever to run in Great Britain. With a grate area of 50 sq ft they were basically as large as any other British passenger-train locomotive and, after having been fitted with a double chimney, No 6234 (not streamlined) broke British records in drawbar horsepower. At normal combustion rates, 3 lb of coal sufficed per drawbar-horsepower hour (Bib. 14). Accessibility of inside mechanism was not admirable. The double chimney became standard for the class.

Some streamline lagging sheets made before World War

II and placed in stock were applied to Duchess-type 'Pacifics' built during the war, but all streamlining was eventually removed, exposing a smokebox distorted in a manner that suggested a survivor of a drunken brawl. This also was corrected later, by substituting plain cylindrical smoke-boxes.

While the various technical factions in the LMS were wrangling (1923–6) over what should be built for the West Coast main-line services, consideration was being given to minor duties and led to two very satisfactory classes of locomotive, the 'Horwich 2/2-6-0' (R82) and the 'Fowler 2/2-6-4T' (R168).

The striking external feature of the 2/2-6-0 was the steep inclination of the cylinders consequent upon the high setting necessary for them to comply with the civil engineer's specification of platform clearance. (Later on Stanier questioned this and it was found to be quite unnecessarily restrictive.) Valves were big enough for mixed-traffic duty, a test figure of 3·3 lb of coal per drawbar-horsepower hour was good, and axleboxes stood up well to their job. A taper-boiler version of the class was produced by Stanier, with higher boiler pressure and smaller cylinders parallel to the rails.

The 2/2-6-4T showed about the same coal rate as the 2/2-6-0 and its valves were large enough to make it a fast runner. With outer-suburban trains running into Euston, these tank engines would go through Willesden at 80 mph and, on a similar job on the Midland main line, one of them was once timed at 90 mph in passing Radlett.

After Stanier had started the taper-boiler era in LMS locomotive affairs, 2-6-4 tank engines similar in general size and proportions to the Fowler 2/2-6-4Ts, but with GW-style boilers, were built for that group in considerable numbers. One class (R173) had three cylinders and was generally employed on the London, Tilbury & Southend line. Most of them, however, were two-cylinder engines and their work was widely spread over the LMS system.

Similarly, 2/2-6-2Ts were built for the LMS in Fowler's time and taper-boiler equivalents were produced by Stanier and by Ivatt.

On the freight side, the most notable LMS locomotives were the thirty-three 'Beyer-Garratt' type 4/2-6-6-2s (R208) designed in collaboration with Beyer-Peacock and built in 1927. These engines were much inferior to what they ought to have been, because Beyer-Peacock were over-ruled by Midland stultification over such things as valves and axleboxes. Each locomotive did the work of the two 0-6-0s that commonly headed each coal train on the Midland main line. The fireman's work on the up-gradients was hard, and, after that had been made clear, rotating coal bunkers were substituted for the original conventional ones so that the coal could be reliably fed to the footplate without manual assistance.

Right until nationalization some 500 0-8-0s (eg, R87) of North Western origin continued to work goods trains on the LMS but in 1935 Stanier introduced a 2/2-8-0 (R102) and subsequently built it in hundreds.

The outstanding product of the Stanier period was the class 5 2/4-6-0 (R53) which was in essence the Great Western 'Hall' class 2/4-6-0 provided with outside Walschaerts valve gear instead of inside Stephenson gear. These engines introduced LMS enginemen to an entirely new idea of what a mixed-traffic engine might be. No other class of locomotive was ever accorded such wholehearted widespread acceptance by shed staff and enginemen as was this. It was rapidly multiplied and was given regular duties into places as widely separated as London, York, Aberdeen, Thurso, Stranraer, Holyhead, Swansea, and Bournemouth.

Oddly enough, the corresponding Stanier 3/4-6-0 'Jubilee' class (R61) introduced a few months after the class 5 was, at first, a very doubtful design, because its 'steaming' was un-reliable. Various alterations were made with the aim of re-moving this fault; it was eventually eliminated by adopting, as a last resort, the engine driver's first resort, which was that of reducing the cross-sectional area of the blast-nozzle. (The same thing was done nearly twenty years later by BR to class 5 2/4-6-os (Bib. 37, p 133).)

Some advantage had been gained by adopting a larger superheater than the original one, because this change increased the total cross-sectional area through which the hot gas from the fire passed through the tubes into the smokebox. Soon afterwards the term 'gas area' began to appear in print.

Before World War II a 'Royal Scot' (No 6170) appeared with a taper boiler and a cylindrical smokebox resting on a saddle and this was in some sense a prototype for 'rebuilds' or 'conversions' of 'Royal Scots'. When those engines were about fifteen years old, recurrent leakage trouble with their old-fashioned wrapper-type smokeboxes suggested the desirability of bringing things a bit nearer to date. So, in 1943, a 'Scot' was 'rebuilt' with different cylinders and with a boiler generally similar to that of No 6170. A double blast-pipe and double chimney were provided and the converted 'Scots' (R62) often developed very considerably more power than did the original 'Scots'. This was convincingly demonstrated in the British Railways 'locomotive exchange' in 1948 when the peak efforts of the 'Converted Scots' were comparable with those of the 'Pacifics'. A Great Western 'King' with double chimney might have done even better but no such engine was available at that time.

Stanier left the LMS in 1944 and his immediate successor, Fairburn, survived only till 1945. From then, till nationalization in 1948, LMS locomotive development was supervised by H. G. Ivatt, son of H. A. Ivatt of Great Northern 'Atlantic' fame. Advances, substantial but undramatic, were made in the valuable direction of designing to minimize day-to-day running costs and long-term maintenance. Churchward methods, modified to match forty years of change in operating conditions, had covered everything else but it had taken the LMS nearly twenty years to get round to them.

CHANGE ON THE LNE

With J. G. Robinson on the Great Central already past the normal retiring age of 65, and with Sir Vincent Raven of the North Eastern not far from it, the obvious choice for the locomotive chieftainship of the newly formed LNE group was the distinctly younger H. N. Gresley, who had shown a markedly progressive spirit while in charge of locomotive affairs on the Great Northern Railway. No subsequent event cast any doubt on the propriety of the appointment and locomotive development on the LNE went on rationally and smoothly from the start until Gresley's death in 1941.

There was no rush to develop a set of LNE standard locomotive designs. Where there was local need for more power it was met by building locomotives of some proved design of one of the constituent companies. For example, a batch of Great Central 'Director' class 4-4-0s were built for southern Scotland as superior alternatives to the North British 4-4-0s. A batch of Great Central 'Coronation Tank' 4-6-2Ts were built for use in the Middlesbrough–Sunderland–Saltburn area. Some 4-6-0s of Great Eastern design were built so that some could be sent to the Great North of Scotland section of the LNE where more power was required within severely restricted axle-loading. This policy was opposed to that of utmost standardization which is technically right, but it diminished any tendency of staff to fear that individuality was to be suppressed in favour of absolute domination from above.

Similarly there was no imposition of an LNE standard for such details as chimneys. It is true that some horrific styles were tried and that they displaced Great Central chimneys which were probably the most refined of all those that came into the LNE group, but later on near-Great Central chimneys replaced some of the early grouping atrocities.

Locomotive design on the LNE was characterized by

maximum use of the three-cylinder principle with Gresley mechanism for the inside valve and by use of wide fireboxes in all the larger locomotives. After their valves and valve gears had been put right the Gresley 'Pacifics' were excellent machines and the Gresley 2-6-2 (R129) was the only successful British design of tender engine with that wheel arrangement.

There was some rebuilding of pre-grouping classes of locomotive, a striking case being that of the GE 4-6-0s (R34) with larger boilers (R35). These were perhaps the best British inside-cylinder 4-6-0s but, as happened with other rebuilds, regular use of the higher power cracked the frames rather too quickly.

Gresley also rebuilt NE 3/4-4-4Ts (R180) to 3/4-6-2Ts (R191) to get more grip on the rails.

The most striking development on the LNE was that of the A4 class, streamlined 'Pacifics' (R119) and streamlined trains beginning with the London–Newcastle 'Silver Jubilee' in 1935. The start-to-stop average between London and Darlington was about 70 mph and, as an average of 600 hp sufficed to pull the normal 230-ton train on this schedule, the job was not difficult for an A4. The London–Edinburgh 'Coronation', introduced in 1937, averaged 71·9 mph to the first stop at York with a load that could be as high as 325 tons. This was one of the hardest regular tasks for British locomotives and even the A4s, with maximum speeds up to 100 mph, had not much to spare.

But most of the work of the thirty-five A4s was done in hauling the heavy main-line passenger trains and they could average a mile a minute over long distances with loads up to 650 tons.

Right the way from 1923 the LNE had favoured 'Pacifics' and plenty of them. They added 3/2-6-2s from 1936 and after World War II they went in for 'Pacifics' with grate areas of 50 sq ft. By the end of 1947 the LNE had some 325 locomotives with grate areas exceeding 40 sq ft while the total for the rest of Great Britain was only 113. This difference was not paralleled in the traffics of the four groups; it represented a difference in general design policy that gave the LNE some 75 'Pacifics' before any other group (apart from the Great Western which scrapped in 1924 its 'Pacific' built in 1908) had any.

Every LNE 'Pacific' had three cylinders and the same feature was also applied by Gresley to smaller locomotives, such as the 3/4-4-0s of class D49 (R27), the 'Sandringham' 3/4-6-0s (R63) and the V1 3/2-6-2Ts (R165). The difficult operating conditions in World War II emphasized that a third cylinder was an undesirable complication in a locomotive and that it should not be included unless there was no alternative.

Gresley's successor, Thompson, recognized this and made tentative steps, in rebuilding a 3/4-4-0 D49 to 4-4-0, 3/2-6-0 K3 to 2/2-6-0, and a 3/4-6-0 B17 to 2/4-6-0, towards substantially reducing the number of three-cylinder engines on the LNE, but this was never achieved.

Considerable numbers of J11 0-6-0s (R4) were rebuilt with piston valves above the cylinders and a noticeably higher pitch of the boiler.

The GC design of 2/2-8-0 (LNE class O4) (R101) was very highly regarded by those who had to run them and keep them running. Nevertheless, many of them were 'rebuilt' with different boilers (of GN design) and with different cylinders having piston valves worked by Walschaerts valve gear.

In 1936 Doncaster produced, as a large mixed-traffic engine the class V2 3/2-6-2 locomotive (R129) that was a K3 at the front and an A3 at the back. It was the only British example of a 2-6-2 tender engine that was good enough to be multiplied.

As a means of countering the difficulties arising out of the uncertain quality of coal available after World War II, most of the 'Pacifics' produced by the LNE after Gresley's death in 1941 had grate areas of 50 sq ft and the Gresley mechanism for the inside valve was abandoned in favour of Walschaerts gear. Because of the bigger grate they were potentially more powerful engines and, had pre-World War II conditions been regained, they might have demonstrated it.

A miscellaneous lot of Thompson-built 'Pacifics' (R121/2) numbering about twenty had the bogie well ahead of the coupled wheels, and the outside cylinders were attached to the frame plates in the space thus made available. Elastic deformation of the frame between the outside cylinders and the smokebox cracked the pipes that fed the outside cylinders and to avoid this a sliding joint was later built into each pipe. With large valves and double chimneys these engines were fast and they scurried very gaily up and down the plain of York with some of the lighter express trains. But none of these post-war designs surpassed the Gresley 'Pacifics', many of which late in their lives were provided with double chimneys and small smoke-lifting wings alongside the smokebox.

CHANGE ON THE GW

The general design plan produced by Churchward in 1901 sufficed for the vast majority of Great Western requirements till 1948. Designs of two-cylinder locomotives were produced from different combinations of standard components and all went into service without difficulty.

Outside the Churchward master-plan lay the four-cylinder 4-6-os and by their outstanding work with the principal passenger trains they delighted the traffic department hardly less than the outside observer. Indeed, in contrast to the indifferent showing of four-cylinder engines on other British railways, they worked so well on the Great Western as to induce that company to build some 250 of virtually one design over a period of about forty years. The explanation is that Great Western design was sound in the basic essentials, which are to provide plenty of space for air, water, and steam to go where they ought to go and to prohibit them from going where they ought not to go and, moreover, to employ such materials and constructions that 50,000 miles of running caused only small departures from this ideal.

But time and again it was shown that what worked well on one railway was not necessarily acceptable on another and copying of the Great Western 'Star' provides an example. In 1916 the Great Southern & Western Railway of Ireland, with locomotive matters under the control of an ex-Great Western engineer, produced a four-cylinder 4-6-0 quite clearly modelled on the Swindon pattern but improved by having its valve gear outside the frame instead of inside it. After World War I nine similar locomotives were built and they ran the most important passenger trains on the GSW main line for some years. But maintenance was found to be expensive and so the engines were rebuilt with only two cylinders which were outside the frame in the conventional position between the bogie wheels.

It is easy to understand that it is less expensive to keep two cylinders in running order than four, but the unbalance of the two-cylinder engine punishes the engine frame, the permanent way, and the bridges more severely than does a four-cylinder engine of equal power. Which is the more expensive overall? The GSW thought it was the four-cylinder engine but the Great Western did not wholly agree.

After the railway grouping of 1923 the Great Western produced a 'Star' enlarged in boiler and cylinders by about 10 per cent and fitted it with a better cab (although still a very draughty one) and called it *Caerphilly Castle*. The same name was applied by the Publicity Department to a handsomely produced book of 200 pages, describing basic principles of steam locomotives, the highlights of Great Western locomotive history and the origin and details of the new design. The book was, deservedly, a tremendous

R135 One of the later versions with welded tanks

R137 Tank tapered to improve driver's view when 'buffering-up'
to a low vehicle

R138 Extensively used on GE London suburban services

R138 GW double-frame saddle-tank built at Swindon in 1879.
Worked till 1938

R141 Tank-engine version of 'Cauliflower' 0-6-0

R142 Designed for South Wales coal traffic. (The 0-6-2T was a favourite on the pre-grouping railways of South Wales)

R144 LNE version of Gresley design of 1920

R149 Jack on running-board (regular LY practice)

R146 Safety valves on dome (regular Drummond practice)

R152 Water-scoop under bunker. Jack on running-board

R155 Early Churchward cast-iron chimney

R161 Bars give extra support to the buffer-beam

R166 Top feed to boiler, header-discharge valve, snifting valve ahead of splasher. Bogie brakes

R168 One of the longest British locomotives. Brakes on all wheels

R177 1932 version of an original design of about 1875. One of this
class touched 80 mph while pushing one coach

R175 Coal carried on top of firebox. No front look-out

R184 Hand-rail, link, and lever to move the superheater damper in the smokebox

R185 'Coronation tank'. First used on suburban passenger trains
out of Marylebone

R197 Shunting engine. Lever reverse (rare on LNW)

R203 Shunting engine, for Feltham yard (Middlesex)

R181 Sometimes called 'Flatirons'. Some derailments at speed led to limitation of the class to slow goods trains

R193 Most successful British 4-6-4. Instability at speed led to addition of a well-tank and drastic reduction of water capacity of side-tanks

R201 Originally designed for South Wales coal traffic and for a long time limited to it

R202 Rebuilt from R201 in 1934 after decline in Welsh coal trade to widen the utility of the engines

R180 Westinghouse pump. Steam reversing gear

R204 Shunting tank. Exhaust quieter than that of corresponding
two-cylinder engine

R205 Four built in 1908 for Wath yard. Two of slightly altered design
in 1932 for Whitemoor (March)

R207 Built to 'prove' calculated acceleration. Boiler pressure had to be
raised from 200 to about 250 psi to do it. James Holden in foreground

success and the fame of the 'Castle' class was established.
For many years afterwards the work of the 'Castles' justified
that fame and did nothing to persuade the public that it was
nonsense to claim, as the *Caerphilly Castle* book had done,
that the 'Castle's' nominal tractive effort of over 31,000 lb
made it 'the most powerful passenger locomotive in Great
Britain'. Tractive effort is not a measure of power. You
cannot measure power in pounds, but when a rival has
affected to do so you miss no chance to outdo him. So, when
the Southern 4/4-6-0 'Lord Nelson' appeared in 1926 with a
nominal tractive effort of 33,000, that locomotive, too, was
claimed to be the most powerful in Britain.

The Great Western was stung by this into quick action and
within a year had recaptured this mythical distinction with a
115 per cent 'Castle' called *King George V*. This took the
classic Great Western four-cylinder 4-6-0 to about its practical limit in size, and a better design might well have been
evolved had more time been allowed for re-examining
fundamentals. To produce the 'King' design every significant
dimension of the 'Castle' had been altered and, by a not-
quite-honest artifice, the nominal tractive effort had been
pushed just over 40,000 lb. The dodge was to quote the
cylinder diameter as 16¼ ins although every 'King' but the first
one started with 16-in cylinders and reached (or surpassed)
16¼ ins only on re-boring to correct wear after many thousands
of miles in service.

An odd and rather fascinating feature of the 'Kings' was
their bogie. Collett wanted 'independent springing' of the
four corners of the bogie as distinct from the conventional
spring-in-equalizing-beam Churchward bogie. But the inside cylinders left inadequate room for inside springs for
the leading axle, while the outside cylinders prohibited
outside springs for the rear axle. So the bogie frame plates
were bent to lie outside the leading wheels and between the
trailing wheels. It is said that the draughtsman who proposed
this solution privately deemed it too absurd to be adopted,

but no objection was raised and it came to give the 'Kings' a visual distinction. But a derailment of one of these bogies suggested inadequately flexible springing and so coiled springs were added 'in series' with the laminated springs.

As a practical demonstration of virtue in the 'Kings' the Paddington–Plymouth time of the famous 'Cornish Riviera Limited' express was reduced from the twenty-year-old figure of 247 minutes to the round four hours.

After 1927 Swindon produced over 500 2/4-6-0s with driving wheels smaller than 6ft 1 ins and brought its total of 2/2-6-0s to nearly 350. None of these showed any appreciable departure from the Churchward design. But what was much more remarkable was the production of about a thousand six-wheel tank engines that owed nothing to Churchward except their 'pannier' tanks attached to the sides of the boiler where they neither obstructed access to the mechanism nor interfered with the fitting of standard chimney, dome and safety valve. No other railway was ever quite so sensible about 0-6-0 tank engines.

In 1939 Swindon did some futile fiddling with wheel diameters of 2/2-6-2Ts and, in 1945, adopted in the 'County' 2/4-6-0s a boiler pressure of 280 psi in order not to be outdone by Bulleid on the Southern, but ventured no other departure from Churchward, and abandoned that freakish boiler pressure soon after the Southern did so.

CHANGE ON THE SOUTHERN

Upon the formation of the Southern Railway in 1923, its motive power was placed under the control of R. E. L. Maunsell, who had been for some ten years the CME of the South Eastern & Chatham line. With technical assistants recruited from Swindon he had given the South Eastern some lively locomotives. His first job on the Southern was to develop out of the LSW 736 class 2/4-6-0 (R48) something more like a Great Western 'Saint'. All that had to be done was to make the valves larger in relation to the cylinders. Reluctant to use very large valves, Maunsell applied valves slightly larger than those of the 736 class to smaller cylinders and put the boiler pressure up to get the nominal tractive effort he wanted. Thus was produced the 'King Arthur' class 2/4-6-0 and no other Southern locomotive was ever bigger and better than this.

After the grouping of railways in 1923, and after a period during which the urgent necessities in motive power had been dealt with, the Southern Railway set out to produce their 'ace' locomotive that should also be a subject for aggressive publicity. This was a four-cylinder 4-6-0 *Lord Nelson* of conventional design (R75) except for an angular setting of the cranks that caused the engine to give eight exhaust beats per revolution of the driving wheels, instead of only four. This made it impossible to balance the reciprocating parts so well as can be done with cranks at right angles, and it led to the use of four sets of valve gear instead of only two plus rocking levers.

In boiler power the 'Nelsons' were about 10 per cent bigger than the two-cylinder 4-6-0s of the Southern 'King Arthur' class 4-6-0s and the Great Western 'Castles', but the normal performance showed nothing like such an advantage and the main reason for this was that the slightness of the slope of the 'Nelson's' long grate made it rather difficult to fire. It was not so bad as the South Western 443 class in this respect, but it was a move in that direction from the well-sloped grate of the 'King Arthur'. There were sixteen 'Nelsons' altogether, and at one time or another some experimental modification of the original design was made to nearly every one of them, a sure sign that the responsible officials were not satisfied with the performance of the engines.

The outstanding Southern Railway locomotive design (R28) was the 'School' class 4-4-0 developed in 1930 to provide higher power for trains on the Hastings route on which the Southern 4-6-0s were not allowed. To produce the 'School', three cylinders of *Lord Nelson* design were used with a shortened version of the 'King Arthur' boiler having a uniformly sloped grate. So capable did the 'Schools' turn out to be that forty were eventually built and undertook some of the hardest jobs on the Southern. They could take 510 tons from Waterloo to Southampton 79·2 miles in 86¼ minutes (Bib. 35) and it was rare for any Southern 4-6-0 to equal this.

The most striking three-cylinder engines on the SR were its first 'Pacifics', the air-smoothed oil-bathed 'Merchant Navy' class, not the least remarkable feature of which was that it was introduced at one of the worst periods in World War II. Sanction for expenditure at that time on what was clearly an express passenger train locomotive is thought to have been extracted on the plea that as 6 ft 2 in wheel diameter was a bit small for a high-speed 'Pacific' these were really to be mixed-traffic engines. For the 280-psi boiler pressure there was no excuse. With larger cylinders 200 psi would have sufficed; even as it was, the engines did most of their work with steam-chest pressure below 200.

The outstanding feature of the Southern 'Pacifics' was the enclosure of the mechanism associated with the inside cylinder and all the valve gear in what was intended to be an oil-tight casing. Compared with normal steam-locomotive practice, in which numerous oil-boxes were filled daily (or more often) with oil that was not recovered, the convenience and economy in lubricating a motor-car engine, simply by 'topping up' the sump, is most striking, and Bulleid made a laudable attempt to achieve the same result in a steam locomotive. But it failed, partly because of the very great and well-known difficulty of preventing oil from escaping along rotating shafts, even in the most favourable conditions, partly because of loss of oil by escape along the piston rod into the cylinder and partly because steam leakage could bring so much water into the oil-bath that parts of the mechanism suffered more corrosion than was common in the conventional exposed mechanism. The Southern 'Pacifics' did, in fact, use much more oil than did conventional three-cylinder locomotives of comparable size. Moreover, oil was plentifully absorbed by the boiler-lagging material and could catch fire to an extent that the local fire-brigade might have to be called to put it out.

Each valve was worked by what was basically Walschaerts gear so laid out that a single crank on a special crankshaft both rocked the expansion link and oscillated the lower end of the combination lever. The resultant motion was not applied directly to the valve-spindle but to the end of an arm on a rocking shaft that was extended into the space between the valve-heads and there provided with an arm linked to a frame that connected them. The valves were arranged for outside admission and the only glands subjected to boiler pressure were those on the piston rods.

The Southern 'Pacifics' were by far the largest locomotives on the Southern Railway and so there was no significance in their ability to do better than the 4-4-os and 4-6-os in ordinary service. This, nevertheless, aroused enthusiasm in some students of locomotive practice, but neither in respect of power in relation to size, nor in useful work per pound of coal, did the Southern 'Pacifics' reach the standards established by the 'Pacifics' of the LNE and of the LMS. They were difficult to maintain in peculiar ways; for example, valve gear was highly stressed and even normal wear of the chain that drove it soon changed the 'valve events'. The multiple exhaust made the beats very quiet but not so markedly so as to conceal their uneven nature. The design included many features designed to save weight and in places this was overdone. At Rugby testing station a Southern 'Pacific' would not give a consistent indicator diagram when running at constant speed and power and this was ascribed to inadequate rigidity of the frame. The flattish top of the smokebox of one of the smaller 'West Country' 'Pacifics' of the same general design was once observed (from an over-bridge) to distend and shrink in synchronism with the exhaust beats as the engine puffed hard up a grade. A 'West Country' created history on September 28th, 1963, (Bib. 30) when, with a ten-coach train, it could not get away from a signal-stop on the curved south-eastern entry to Shrewsbury and so the train had to be 'banked' on the level into the station. (The enginemen's union had insisted that on this trip the engine should not be driven by anyone who knew anything about her.)

Oddities of this kind were to be expected in any machine that included marked departure from convention, but the sad thing is that the Southern 'Pacifics', with all their unsatisfactory features, were produced to a total of over 140, fantastically beyond the possible needs of the Southern Railway for locomotives of their size. One could see two 'Pacifics' on a two-coach train and it was not uncommon to send a 'Pacific' from Exeter to 'shunt the yard' at Okehampton. Incidents of this sort inevitably dimmed the 'image' of the original Southern 'Pacifics' but even the true general picture thoroughly justified the action of British Railways in rebuilding many of them as straightforward three-cylinder 'Pacifics' with no streamlining, no oil-baths, and no nonsense. In this form they were very much more satisfactory in service; they were good, but not outstanding British 'Pacifics'.

During the locomotive exchanges in 1948 a Southern 'Pacific' of the smaller or 'West Country' size distinguished herself and her driver by speeds and power outputs well above the demands of the timetable on widely separated routes in Great Britain. One episode was a climb by a 'West Country' assisted by a Scottish 4-4-0 at such a rate that the boiler pressure of the 4-4-0 dropped markedly or, as it was said, the engine 'ran out of breath'. Admirers of the Southern 'Pacifics' interpreted this as a tribute to the 'West Country' but others thought that it proved only that the 4-4-0 had done more than its fair share of the work.

CHAPTER SEVEN

BRITISH STEAM IN ACTION

SOME HIGHLIGHTS

AT THE beginning of the twentieth century, development of the steam locomotive in Britain was proceeding in size and power rather than in speed. The competition in 1895 between the West Coast and East Coast routes from London to Aberdeen had shown locomotives to be able to run for long distances much faster than ordinary passenger services required and no British railway timetable in 1900 was offering speeds appreciably higher than had its predecessor in 1895. But heavier rolling stock was being built and more people were travelling, and so harder work was required of the engines without trying to go any faster.

The feat of the North Western 2-4-0 *Hardwicke*, in averaging 67 mph start-to-stop from Crewe to Carlisle over Shap Summit in 1895, had shown what speed was practicable with a locomotive pulling about 2½ times its own weight, and some years had to elapse before this kind of thing was done any better.

In 1903 and 1904 Great Western 4-4-0s of the 'City' class showed that they could pull about three times their own weight at 75 mph continuously on the level or over moderate undulations. The Great Western 4-2-2 *Duke of Connaught* averaged 80 mph over 66 miles of very slightly favourable track from passing Shrivenham to passing Ealing with a load of about three times its own weight (Bib. 20). In pure speed the Great Western was leading the rest of Britain and it continued to do so for some thirty years. Nor was its eminence only in speed, for the Churchward 2/4-6-0s and

4/4-6-os coped with continually increasing loads till the interested amateur could judge from published information that they were ahead of all British competitors in power; by 1925 it seemed that they were also ahead in work obtained from each pound of coal.

On the North Western the 4-4-os and 4-6-os built by Whale, and their superheated forms developed by Bowen-Cooke, took heavier all-the-year round passenger trains than ran elsewhere in Britain and a train seven times as heavy as the engine was not unusual even on the principal passenger services. North Western locomotives chattered cheerfully along the main line, throwing sparks in a manner magnificently wasteful and giving the fireman plenty to do, but the company nevertheless paid its shareholders generous dividends (although derived, of course, mostly from goods traffic). The engines themselves, neat in shining black, epitomized the Victorian austerity of F. W. Webb himself, late King of Crewe. When the 4/4-6-0 *Sir Gilbert Claughton* appeared in 1913, many North Western admirers' hearts were stirred to their depths by this impressive embodiment of North Western styling in a really big engine for its time. Occasionally the work of 'Claughtons' was as outstanding as their appearance, but generally they could not be relied upon to equal the best performances of their smaller predecessors on the North Western.

Before 1915, booked average speeds up to about 56 mph were common on the North Western. Maxima as high as 80 mph were rare south of Lancaster, and even north of that point they were less frequent than in earlier years when engines that could not keep time uphill were consequently 'let go' on the downs. Mr C. J. Allen remarked that, in his experience, the North Western was the British railway above all others on which engine drivers would set out to regain time lost by other people. This was achieved by dint of remorseless thrashing of engines which were consequently expensive in maintenance.

Between London and Sheffield the Great Central and the Midland were in direct competition and ran fast trains of weight well within the capacity of the engines, in the first case because only light traffic was offering itself and in the second case because an extra engine was provided for any train that was even a shade heavier than the lenient rules allowed. For passenger trains the Midland used nothing larger than 4-4-0s; the Great Central tried 4-4-2s and 4-6-0s but none was so good as the 'Director' class 4-4-0 introduced in 1913. On both these undulating routes to the north, average speeds were of the same order as on the North Western, but maxima over 80 mph were common; now and again there was a near-ninety on the Great Central.

On the Great Northern, the average performance of the Ivatt 'large Atlantics' was hardly so good as might have been expected from their dimensions, or from the part that they were given in Great Northern publicity when the class was introduced. (A contemporary comment was 'No 251, bigger-boilered than ever, leers at us from every hoarding'.) A marked improvement followed the application of superheaters to these engines, but even then no performance before World War I gave any hint of the work that some drivers would thrash out of them on the Great Northern main line after 'Pacifics' had shown there what could be done with really heavy trains. Speeds high in the 'eighties' were often recorded on the downhill stretches from Hitchin to Huntingdon (27 miles) and from Stoke Box, 19 miles southwards to Werrington Junction near Peterborough. In special competition with the Midland, the Great Northern ran an up-and-down 'Leeds Flyer' non-stop between London and Wakefield (175·7 miles). Its lightness (120 to 150 tons) made it, however, an easy train to work and for some years it was indeed run by Stirling 2-2-2s built in the 1880s.

On the Great Eastern, good work was done (especially with heavy trains in the holiday season) by the Holden 'Claud Hamilton' 4-4-0s (original form of R18). Besides handling the long-distance trains on the Great Eastern, these engines ran trains in very lively fashion over the undulations between Liverpool St and Southend in competition with 2/4-4-2Ts (R156) on the flatter Tilbury line from Fenchurch Street. S. D. Holden won about 25 per cent more power when he stretched the 'Claud' design into the 1500 class 4-6-0 (R34) with a bigger cab still.

The 1500s were at home on the 'Norfolk Coast' express that had taxed the 'Clauds' to the limit, but even the 4-6-0s had to be worked hard to keep time with the boat train over 69 miles between Liverpool St and Harwich at 50·5 mph with loads over 400 tons (Bib. 21).

The most striking running of North Eastern engines was achieved on the nearly level 44·1 miles between York and Darlington but, with normal loads, the 'Atlantics' had not to be spurred to any outstanding efforts to keep time. A notable exception was when 3/4-4-2 No 732 (R112) took 545 tons from York to Darlington in 50·3 minutes start-to-stop, averaging 57·5 mph over the very slight ascent of 36 miles from Beningbrough to Croft Spa (Bib. 22). More in the public eye was the 'fastest train in the British Empire' booked to average 61·6 mph from Darlington to York. This was normally a train of less than 180 tons handled by a 4-4-0 of class R. No 1672 of this class once made the run in 39 min 34 sec and this was the 'record' for many years. (It was startling to read even in 1967 that a diesel-electric locomotive had covered the distance in ten minutes less than this!)

On every weekday in the summer of 1914 over 200 trains in Britain ran more than 100 miles without a stop. More than half these runs were repeated in the summer of 1915 but thereafter World War I took a severe toll and the first serious moves back towards pre-war service did not occur till September 1921. In the *Railway Magazine* for December 1921 Mr C. J. Allen described a rousing run with a Great Western 'Star' on the down 'Limited', and every reader was then convinced that the war was over. For in a distance of 130 miles the engine gained *sixteen minutes* on one of the fastest schedules in Great Britain. This tended to convince even those who could not conveniently examine confirmatory evidence in earlier issues of the *Railway Magazine* that, whenever an occasion justified it, Churchward locomotives could show themselves able to beat all others in Britain in 'pulling' or 'running' or anything else. The running of the 'Castles' (R66) in 1924 and 1925 convinced professional engineers about this and, ten years later, locomotives of Churchward quality were no longer peculiar to the Great Western Railway.

A paper presented by Collett to the 1924 World Power Conference reported 'Castle' coal consumption on test as 2·83 lb per drawbar-horsepower hour. Many locomotive engineers at first dismissed this as far too good to be true, but Gresley took it seriously after his 'Pacifics' were decisively beaten by 'Castles' in the locomotive exchange of 1925, and in special tests in 1927 the LNE recorded 3·11 lb per drawbar-horsepower hour by a 'Pacific' working at 220 psi and slightly less by a similar locomotive at 180 psi (Bib. 12).

Reduction in coal consumption of Gresley 'Pacifics' by correction of the original error in valve design made it possible for one to take a train all the way between London and Edinburgh in eight hours. The corridor tender, introduced in 1928 to enable the enginemen to be changed without stopping, was an absurd 'gimmick' and especially so because elimination of the corridor would have permitted a useful enlargement of the coal capacity of the tender. Perhaps this was not important for the leisurely running of the 'Flying Scotsman' in 1928 and indeed for some time afterwards, but British railways speeds in general were showing a slow upward trend, while loads were still tending to increase.

The year 1932 brought some marked acceleration of a number of principal passenger services and one of them gave the LMS 5.25 PM Liverpool (Lime St) to Euston train a time of 142 minutes start-to-stop for the 152·6 miles from Crewe to Willesden Junction. 'Royal Scots' (R59) were required to achieve this average of 64·5 mph with loads up to 350 tons, and, with engines kept in specially good condition for the job, it was well done. A report (Bib. 15) on seven runs showed No 6105 to have made the trip in 133·3 minutes net with 320 tons. On one occasion the driver (*not* the fireman this time) showed exceptional skill in arriving at Willesden within 12 seconds of scheduled time, in being nowhere more than 34 seconds away from booked time and in nowhere exceeding 78 mph.

Ever since 1923 the Great Western had scheduled a daily train from Swindon to Paddington at over 61 mph and, by the late summer of 1932, had cut its time down to 65 minutes, representing 71·3 mph. In a special effort on June 5th, 1932, a 'Castle' No 5006 ran this 'Cheltenham Flyer' (195 tons on that day) from Swindon to London at 81·3 mph start-to-stop, a record never beaten in Britain by steam over any distance. The maximum speed was 92 mph at Didcot, Goring and Tilehurst (Bib. 16).

Until September 1939 the train ran five days a week and usually the net time (with allowance for any delay) was kept or bettered with loads up to 270 tons. On some occasions the net time was less than the record-breaking 56 min 47 sec of 1932. But one of the most remarkable efforts by the locomotive on this train was made by 'Castle' No 5023 in taking 430 tons over the course in a net time of 66¼ minutes (Bib. 17). There were other runs on which the driver showed his mastery of the job by keeping time without exceeding 77 mph anywhere.

The very high booked speed of this one daily train over the Swindon–Paddington route was very largely a publicity-based showpiece. A normal run produced no speed higher than could be recorded on other British trains and although the riding of the coaches was not specially smooth, east of Reading, no exceptional risk was taken.

BLITHE SPIRITS

There is a natural interest in the highest speed attained, even momentarily, by anything, and the Great Western held for thirty years the British rail record in this respect by a speed of about 100 mph attained by a double-frame 4-4-0 after running three miles down gradients between 1 in 80 and 1 in 127 near Wellington (Somerset). This was reported in certain newspapers at the time (Bib. 23).

What received no such publicity, and was never admitted officially for some thirty years, was the attainment of about 120 mph by Great Western 2/4-6-0 (R37), No 2903, whilst running without a train between Badminton and Wootton Bassett in May 1906 (Bib. 24). It is hard to think of any technical justification for this undoubtedly risky proceeding (normal balance-weights would lift the driving wheels of such an engine from the rails eight times per second at that speed) and, as there were a number of highly placed technical staff from Swindon on the footplate, one is inclined to suggest that someone had 'dared' someone else to take part in it. This may seem absurd, but even less commendable things were done on British railways over thirty years later.

Perhaps the most dramatic incident in the development of British steam occurred on September 27th, 1935, shortly before the introduction by the LNE of a 'streamlined train' running daily once in each direction between Newcastle and King's Cross.

Special diesel-engined trains of a few coaches had been running in Germany at start-to-stop average speeds over 70 mph and the LNE had decided that a rather heavier train could be taken at such speeds by a Gresley 'Pacific'. It was also decided to introduce such a train with special features that the public might find attractive in addition to its high speed. So the Gresley 'Pacific' design was modified to have smaller cylinders and larger valves, bringing the general proportions and the 'nominal speed' in fact right into the Churchward class. To secure a nominal tractive effort appropriate for hauling 600-ton trains at 60 mph, with the largest cylinders that the Gresley layout permitted with central setting of the inside cylinder, the boiler pressure was pushed up to 250 psi. The locomotive was enclosed in a sheet-steel casing that 'streamlined' the leading end and the special train built for the new service was similarly treated.

Passengers, including journalists, were invited to join the train on a special run from King's Cross to Grantham. The new engine (*Silver Link*) was opened out with its 'feather-weight' load of 220 tons, and 75 mph was found to be its comfortable speed up 1 in 200. Over 43 miles of downhill and level it averaged 100 mph. The coaches, suspended in a manner not previously tried out at such a speed, gave a ride that repeatedly terrorized those passengers with knowledge and imagination, but no one was hurt. Peterborough, 76·4 miles out, was passed at low speed in 55 minutes from King's Cross and, if the train had stopped there, it would have set up a British steam record of 82·5 mph for a start-to-stop run over any distance. Beyond Peterborough there were delays from a regular train that had left London three-quarters of an hour before the special did.

The 'Silver Jubilee' train ran five days a week for four years at a booked average speed of 70·3 mph between King's Cross and Darlington. A similar train, the 325-ton 'Coronation', ran (1937–9) between London and Edinburgh in six hours with two intermediate stops (71·9 mph from London to York) and another averaged 68 mph between King's Cross and Leeds. Speed was nominally limited to 90 mph but even 100 mph was occasionally exceeded and, in a special effort (August 26th, 1936) of which the Press had been told, a maximum of 113 mph was reached by A4 'Pacific' No 2512 in descending from Stoke Summit to Peterborough.

South of Peterborough the big-end of the inside connecting-rod failed, but the train kept going with increasing damage and reached the final descent from Potter's Bar before the inside cylinder-ends were knocked out. Steam had to be applied to reach the buffer-stops at King's Cross and so Britain's first two-cylinder 'Pacific' did her first job with steam roaring from under her clothing. No one was hurt.

By the time the LMS had acquired streamlined 'Pacifics' in 1937 someone thought that they might try to beat 113 mph. This was done officially with barely credible recklessness. The attempt was made on the sharply downhill stretch between Madeley and Crewe and afterwards the brakes were applied with the train running at more that 100 mph, with only two miles of falling grade before reaching the junctions at the south end of Crewe Station. Not even the precaution had been taken of preparing a run right through the station on the route with least curvature. The train was scheduled to swerve on to a platform line and to stop in the station. This it did, but only just, passengers being flung off their feet by violent side movements of the coaches on an S-bend in the approach to the platform. A top speed of 114 mph had been touched near mile-post 156 and then trust had to be placed on prayer, luck, and a full brake application. No one was badly hurt, and the engine shortly afterwards took the train back to Euston at an average of 79·7 mph.

This episode emphasized that brakes were more important than locomotives and that not enough was known about their limitations at high speeds.

Although there is no perceptible curvature of the LNE main line for several miles below the top-speed point on Essendine bank, the LNE decided against any public participation in its reply to the Madeley bank frolic but invited Mr C. J. Allen, at that time in its employ, to join the train. Having survived *Silver Link*'s maiden effort, No 2512's self-eviscerating escapade on the LNE main line and *Coronation*'s savage lurch into Crewe, however, he felt that luck had its

limits and so declined on the plea of 'Not on Sunday'. In
the event, double-chimney A4 'Pacific' No 4468 *Mallard*
came over Stoke Summit with 230 tons at 75 mph and was
driven 'all out' down the bank past Essendine with a momentary maximum of 126 mph, unequalled elsewhere in Britain
and barely matched by a big 4-6-4 in Germany. No one was
hurt and very little rehabilitation sufficed to enable *Mallard*
to re-enter normal service. There was no rejoinder from the
LMS which had no long downhill and run-out like Essendine
bank.

Special efforts to reach very high speeds, although exciting
for the enthusiast, interesting to the general public, and
(perhaps) enlightening to the engineer, were not very useful
to the railways generally. What was more important, on the
passenger side, was the general level of speed maintained in
regular service. In the summer of 1939 there were in Britain
daily scheduled runs totalling 12,000 miles at over a mile a
minute. These included 730 miles at over 70 mph.

Very high standards of locomotive performance were
being maintained on the 'best' express passenger trains on
the two largest railway groups by 'Pacifics', on the Great
Western by 4-6-0s and on the Southern most notably by
3/4-4-0s. But even so, most of the revenue was won by
0-6-0s, 0-8-0s, and 2-8-0s on goods and mineral trains.

The 'locomotive exchanges' effected by British Railways
in 1948 produced no real surprises, after allowances had
been made for the inevitable ranges of uncertainty about the
numerical results. The producers of greatest power in relation
to size were the double-chimney 'Rebuilt Scots' (R62) and
they confirmed that, at least for journeys up to about 200
miles, 4-6-0s could meet all British needs.

The 1939 standards of steam-locomotive operation in
Britain were never quite reattained (Appendix 3 is nearly all
pre-1940) partly because the need for them was avoided by
building lots of big engines. Nevertheless, after about 1959,
peak speeds over 100 mph became more common than they

had been before 1940. Classes of locomotive that reached
that speed included:

GW	'City' 4-4-0 (in 1904)
	'Saint' 2/4-6-0 (in 1906)
	'Castle' 4/4-6-0
	'King' 4/4-6-0
LMS	'Coronation' 4/4-6-2
	'Rebuilt Scot' 3/4-6-0
LNE	Classes A1 A3 A4 3/4-6-2 (Gresley)
	Class A1 3/4-6-2 (Peppercorn)
	Class A2/3 3/4-6-2 (Thompson)
SR	'Merchant Navy' 3/4-6-2
BR	'Britannia' 2/4-6-2

This list is not claimed to be exhaustive. With the ap-
proaching end of steam on certain routes, there were some
astonishing 'last flings' by all kinds of locomotives.

OBSERVATION BY PASSENGERS

Although, as we have seen, the bulk of railway haulage was
done by unpretentious six-wheel locomotives, and although
the work of the most dramatic flyer on an express passenger
train can be assessed by a single number and although the
cost of doing such work cannot be ascertained with any
approach to precision, the railway enthusiast does like to
read details, significant or not, about the running of engines.
How many such details have been obtained without official
sanction will never be known; official permission for anyone
but professional enginemen to ride on locomotives was only
rarely given and every published report by an approved
rider had first to go through a fine official filter. Two early
reports (Bib. 18 and 19) of this character by Mr C. J. Allen
were of exceptional interest, firstly because they referred to

the running of the two premier British main-line locomotives of the period (a Gresley 'Pacific' and a Great Western 'Castle'), secondly because they showed what seemed to be a marked difference in operating methods, and thirdly because the 'Pacific' (LNE 4473) afterwards became distinguished in at least two ways. (With 180-psi boiler pressure, she equalled a 220-psi 'Pacific' in coal consumption (Bib. 12); with 395 tons she ran 141 miles at 74·4 mph (Bib. 34).)

The 'Pacific' handled one of the hardest LNE jobs of the time (440/480 tons from Doncaster to King's Cross with stops at Retford, Grantham, and Peterborough) without difficulty. The boiler pressure was allowed to vary and never quite reached the 'blowing-off' figure of 180 psi. The cut-off was at 45 per cent for most of the way; over a short easy stretch it was 40 per cent.

This was in 1923, a few months before the appearance of the first Great Western 4/4-6-0 of the 'Castle' class, which was Churchward's 'Star' enlarged by about 10 per cent. The known abilities of the 'Stars' caused enthusiasts to look forward eagerly to any scrap of information about the work of the 'Castles'. The very first published hint might have been derived from a picture in the *Railway Magazine* for July 1924 of No 4079 *Pendennis Castle* running the down 'Cornish Riviera' express along the coast between Dawlish Warren and Dawlish with no one in the driver's normal position on the footplate. This might mean that the driver was firing to give some relief to an exhausted fireman, or it might mean that the job was so easy that the driver had gone over to the other side to share the sea breezes with the fireman. You just could not tell, and you almost wished you had not noticed anything out of the ordinary in the picture.

The first account of the work of the 'Castles' was Mr Allen's description of a ride on No 4079 hauling the 'Cornish Riviera' express from London to Plymouth, with about the heaviest loading it had had up to that time and on a schedule that made the first 70 miles the hardest regular task ever set to any British locomotive in relation to its size. (Over that stretch it was sensible and not unusual to lose time, as it could easily be recovered later in the journey, but with a visitor and an inspector on board, you worked to the book even if it killed you.)

The run was made in October on a perfect day, apart from thickish mist in the first few miles. In the *Railway Magazine* for December 1924 a Mackay photograph of the start from Paddington showed No 4079's copper-capped chimney gleaming through the mist with a knowing smile. She was about to run non-stop through 200 miles of autumnal splendour and to show the visitor on her footplate British locomotive performance at the highest level it ever attained. With fourteen vehicles, weighing 530 tons loaded, she roared through Slough at 69 mph, slowed to 45 for the left turn at Reading, picked up to 62 mph in the flatter part of the Kennett valley, and then climbed its steepening gradient, amid a succession of picturesque views of lush countryside right up to the top near Savernake Forest without falling below 48 mph and without any cut-off later than 30 per cent. Compared with 4473's normal 45 per cent, this read like child's play and one could have imagined almost noiseless running of the 'Castle'. There was, however, a remark about 'her pretty beat' even on the level and, in fact, there was probably a crisp crackle from the chimney as she went through Savernake. To cover 70 miles horizontally and 415 ft vertically upwards in $73\frac{1}{2}$ minutes, with a gain in speed from zero to 48 mph and a reduction from 65 to 45 at Reading, was equivalent to running continuously at about 65 mph on the level. With 530 tons this meant an average of 1,100 horsepower at the drawbar and this in turn meant burning coal at the rate of about 55 lb per minute.

As the fireman would certainly be following the general Great Western practice of pulling up the flap-plate in front of the firehole after each shovelful of coal, he could have seen very little of the beauties of Berkshire on this tip. He had some chance of viewing the transition from heavily wooded country to bare downs on the easy 25 miles to West-bury where the train had covered 97½ miles in as many minutes from the start. The loss of two coaches for Wey-mouth by 'slipping' at Westbury brought the load down to 450 tons and, after climbing a sharp rise to a summit 108½ miles from Paddington, No 4079 had a pretty easy time in going down into Somerset and across the marshes near Athelney to pass Taunton (142·9 miles) in 144·4 minutes. There the speed of 60 mph made a lively entry onto the climb that ends with 2½ miles or so at 1 in 85 and another at 1 in 127 through the Whiteball tunnel. On this stretch, 10·9 miles were covered, and the train (now of 385 tons after slipping coaches at Taunton) was lifted 300 ft in 14 minutes. This re-quired 830 drawbar-horsepower and a coal feed of about 40 lb per minute if the fire were to lose no depth during this period.

At Whiteball Summit everyone relaxed as the curves in the next 40 miles prohibit the speed that anything like hard work would produce. Entry into Devonshire makes this truly West Country, with pinkish stone quarries at Burlescombe and gradually reddening earth on the way down the valley to Exeter. With all the colours of autumn presented in gay sequence and the engine hardly pulling the train, this must have been a most delightful part of the journey. Even the fireman had a chance to enjoy it.

After slipping the Kingswear coaches at Exeter, No 4079 had only 275 tons to handle and found it easy to keep the schedule time of 24 minutes for the 20 miles of Exe-estuary, seashore, and Teign-bank to Newton Abbot. A couple of miles farther on, house-roof gradients begin and, for the first time, cut-off was advanced well beyond 30 per cent to get up the steepest pitches. But the fire was still clean and there was no trouble about keeping boiler pressure close to the 'blowing-off' point. Plymouth was reached almost casually three minutes early in 244 minutes for the 225·7 miles.

Coal consumption for the journey was visually estimated at

about $3\frac{1}{2}$ tons corresponding to 35 lb per mile. This, in conjunction with No 4079's cut-off generally below 30 per cent compared with No 4473's minimum of 40 per cent for what was probably a smaller average power output, suggested much more economical running by the 'Castle' than by the 'Pacific'. Various explanations could be imagined for this and the most popular one was that the 225-psi boiler pressure of the 'Castle' made for higher efficiency than the 180 psi of the 'Pacific'. The possible gain by virtue of the higher pressure is actually too small to be detectable with certainty in any quantitative test, and, in fact, it never has been detected. The only real explanation deducible from published dimensions was that the valves of the 'Pacific' were not large enough to permit of the highest possible cylinder efficiency when working hard at speed.

In 1925 'Castles' and Gresley 'Pacifics' ran in comparative tests on GW and LNE trains with the object of ascertaining which class of locomotive could do the work on the smaller quantity of coal. The result confirmed the conclusion suggested by Mr Allen's reports of his footplate trips. It moved Doncaster into examination of valve events, and a simple rearrangement of valves and valve gear on Gresley 'Pacifics' brought their coal consumption down by an extent that would probably have given them the victory in the 1925 exchange had it been applied in time.

It seems likely that it was the comparison between the cut-off figures quoted by Mr Allen for No 4473 and No 4079 that started off what became the 'cut-off craze' which ran to almost incredible absurdities. Every footplate rider bent on publication recorded readings of the cut-off indicator and possibly assumed (as some readers of accounts certainly did) that each reading represented the actual cut-off. In most cases it did not because:

(1) Slackness in the joints in the valve gear allowed the actual valve-travel to differ from that of a valve worked by perfect mechanism and set at the same cut-off

reading. The travel was short at low speed and long
at high speed.

(2) Build-up of carbon on the valve and the steam-chest
liner could cause the effective port opening to be
markedly less than that of the same valve and steam-
chest liner in the clean condition corresponding to
published dimensions.

Moreover, the reading of the cut-off indicator might be
different from that corresponding to the position of the
die-block that defined the nominal valve-travel.

Consequently one could find a locomotive happily pulling
forwards with the cut-off indicator suggesting backward
gear. One could read of locomotives of the same class doing
identical work, one with a cut-off reading of 15 per cent and
the other of 35 per cent. In spite of numerous comparisons
of this sort it still remained a tradition to publish cut-off
indicator readings as if they meant something.

The routine that came to be established for a footplate
rider included noting passing times and speeds at numerous
points on the route (better done from a seat in the train),
recording cut-off indicator readings, and, even less significant,
noting visual estimates of the position of the regulator
handle. All this kept the observer busy but it left him little
opportunity of recording what the enginemen did. Examination of this section of the literature of the locomotive reveals
a sad tale of lost opportunities now never to be regained.

It may be remarked that some of the most enterprising
drivers could not tell you afterwards what regulator opening
or cut-off they had used in making a lively run. They judged
the engine's effort by the sound of its exhaust and this is
rational inasmuch as it suggests how fast steam is being used
and how hard the fire is being urged. Accurate measure of
of the steam pressure at the blast-pipe was a quantitative
refinement of listening and it was the basis of a most successful locomotive-testing procedure developed at Swindon under
the guidance of Mr S. O. Ell (Bib. 9).

POWER OUTPUT IN RELATION TO SIZE

In trying to estimate the power that a locomotive might develop at the drawbar at the back of its tender it is useful to think, not only of its capacity to develop power, but also of the restrictions that might be placed on it.

First of all an upper limit, although not at all a precise one, was imposed by the rate of heat generation in the firebox. This was limited by the rate at which air was drawn through the fire-bed. The faster it went the hotter the fire, but the bigger were the biggest bits of coal that were lifted up to the tubes and (if they were wide enough) through them. The stronger the draughts the bigger the loss of unburned coal into the smokebox and perhaps through the chimney. But for any given air-speed the greater the grate area, the higher the air-rate per minute and so the greater the amount of heat generated per minute. It was, in fact, proportional to the grate area for a given draught and a given uniform depth of fire-bed.

Strong draught was induced by adopting a blast-nozzle of sufficiently small diameter, and this raised the blast-pipe pressure and consequently the back pressure on the pistons. Conversely, the power of the locomotive might be limited not to what the fire was capable of producing but by the draught that might be produced by the blast. This depended not only on the size of the blast-nozzle but also on the resistance opposed to the draught by restriction of air-flow through the ashpan and the fire, and by drag on the hot gases as they passed through the tubes. The front-end (ie, the blast-pipe, chimney, and smokebox) might be designed to produce draught for large power output in which case it might be limited by the grate area. Otherwise the draughting arrangements themselves might set the limit. It is difficult to make any very accurate estimate of the other factors, but grate area may be accepted as a basic measure of the sustained power of the locomotive although it was actually one of several limitations.

At any time the driver might set a limit to the power output by partly closing the regulator and/or reducing the travel of the valves; ie, making the 'cut-off' earlier. This latter could be a serious restriction in locomotives with flat valves and indeed in many with piston valves. If the valves were small in relation to the cylinder volume then the restriction to steam-flow past the valves meant that, at its normal running speed, the engine could not use all the steam that its boiler could produce without adopting such a late cut-off that the steam was used wastefully in the cylinders. Best performance of the valves was obtained at speeds between 30 per cent and 60 per cent of the 'nominal speed', which is about 1,100 DVL/d^2s. Highest cylinder efficiency was obtained at speeds between 50 and 70 times G/t when the horsepower developed at the pistons was 45 times the grate area, which corresponded to a pretty brisk draught on the fire. (See Appendix 2 for meanings of symbols.) Ideal design set both these speed-ranges in the middle of the range of running speed over which the maximum power was required in service. With flat valves this ideal was hardly ever achieved because, with width of port about equal to the cylinder diameter (usual practice), the ideal 'lap' of the valve for fast running was impracticable. With piston valves a port-width much greater than the cylinder diameter was practicable (and common) but many locomotives had less than the ideal product of diameter and lap of the valves. (See Appendix 2.) By the late 1930s this was becoming more widely appreciated and the standard designs developed after nationalization of the railways in 1948 were generally satisfactory in this respect.

In general, the hardest regular duty assigned to any class of locomotive was within the capacity of an average member of the class, in an average condition of mechanical adjustment and internal cleanliness by average enginemen with average coal. If, on a particular occasion, every feature had its best possible value and the enginemen had an interest and will to do their best, the power output could be 50 or more per cent higher than the normal requirement. Consequently, a close observer of many performances by locomotives of a particular class might distinguish a wide variety in power output without any reason obvious to him. Because of this there grew up a tendency to regard the steam locomotives as unpredictable and to allow the heart to warm to it on that account. Like anything else, it was unpredictable by anyone who either did not have the facts on which to base a prediction, or did not know how to use them to that end. The limit of power of the larger locomotives was never shown because the fireman could not work hard enough to keep it up for long, unless he were a strong intelligent man with a strong incentive. Between his top limit and the average performance of an average fireman there was a wide gap, somewhere in which most performances lay, and any near the upper boundary tended to appear miraculous to the enthusiastic amateur. In fact, big efforts were rare, largely because most enginemen believed that what was occasionally shown to be possible might come to be required regularly. There were, of course, among drivers a few lively characters who enjoyed running hard even to the extent of doing some of the firing if they could not persuade the official fireman to work harder than he was paid to do. Most locomotives in good condition would develop much higher power than ordinary schedules demanded, given the right men in the right mood. It required not skill so much as a combination of determination, physique, and indifference to the wear and tear of the engine.

To measure the useful power output of a locomotive, with any approach to precision, a dynamometer car was required. This meant that it simply could not be done in ordinary service. Although any railway traveller might measure the speed of the train if he had a watch, no passenger could

directly measure the power that the locomotive was developing. If the train was being hauled up a known gradient at
low speed, the power required could be estimated very
closely because it was nearly all being applied to lift the train
and this could be accurately calculated from the speed and the
weight. But if the train were not moving slowly, then an
appreciable fraction of the power might be being dissipated
in bearing friction, wheel-flange friction, and windage.
These effects could be estimated (by formulae for 'train
resistance') but they had wider ranges of uncertainty than has
the effect of gravity.

The figures given in Appendix 3 for drawbar horsepower
were based on the Johansen formula and, although this
rather overestimated the resistance of British Railways
coaching stock, it was not far out for some earlier British
vehicles and it was a reasonable basis for comparison. A great
deal of arithmetical work showed that the drawbar horsepower sustained by a locomotive, divided by the grate area,
gave figures that correlated with duration of efforts and that
suggested a level of performance that a number of classes of
locomotives had attained when working hard in ordinary
service.

That level was reached when over a period of M minutes
the drawbar horsepower per square foot of grate area was:

$$37(M+3)/(M+1)-M/30$$

This works out at 74 for a minute, 49 for 5 minutes, 43 for
10 minutes and so on down to 31 for 200 minutes which
represents about the limit of the data on which the formula
is based.

As the limit of uncertainty is certainly not less than $\pm 2\frac{1}{2}$
per cent, it would be misleading to quote figures of merit in
steps smaller than about 5 per cent. So the 'high-class
standard' was graded at 20. The grade of any particular
performance is the nearest whole number to twenty times the

drawbar horsepower per square foot of grate divided by the figure given by the formula for the duration concerned.

The creation of this method of comparison was possible only by use of the vast amount of information published between 1900 and 1954 by the *Railway Magazine* under the title 'British Locomotive Practice and Performance' after collection and presentation partly by Charles Rous-Marten but mostly by Mr C. J. Allen.

Appendix 3 is a condensate of the gist of some two million figures in over seven-hundred articles published over a period of nearly sixty years about the running of locomotives in normal service as distinct from special test runs. It is substantially the same as a table published in the *Railway Magazine* for July 1956 (p 450) but with certain excisions and modifications made in the light of later examination of the information.

The examples quoted in Appendix 3 constitute only a minute fraction of the total number of published records, which themselves are only a small fraction of privately recorded runs, which in turn represent probably less than one per cent of all the runs made by important express passenger trains. So it is most unlikely that any of the performances recorded in Appendix 3 represents the best ever produced by the class of locomotive concerned. Appendix 3 need not restrain anyone from believing that his favourite class of locomotive was superior to all others, but never happened to demonstrate it when being timed by anyone who submitted his figures for publication.

Comment on 'Thrashing' or 'Flogging'

Although it was common to build and to sell stationary steam engines and marine steam engines guaranteed to develop specified 'horsepower', this was never the practice in respect of steam locomotives. Each was built to do a range of jobs, none of which was associated with any precisely defined horsepower, without throwing too many cinders out of the chimney. If, in special circumstances, an engine was worked much harder than usual (by adopting a late 'cut off' with well-opened regulator) it was said to be being 'thrashed'. This was only a relative term, as what might be regarded as thrashing on one line might be normal on another. But, the harder an engine was worked, the faster it threw solid matter out of its chimney; pushed to absurdity, thrashing might lift coal out of the firebox faster than the fireman could feed it in. There is no fundamental borderline between thrashing and not-thrashing; arbitrarily one may state that an engine was being thrashed if it was getting rid of coal, by burning and ejection, at a rate higher than $2\frac{1}{2}$ lb of coal per square foot of grate area per minute.

In another sense an engine was thrashed if it was using steam uneconomically in its cylinders. Here again no natural borderline exists; arbitrarily one might regard a locomotive as being thrashed if its pull on the train exceeded half its nominal tractive effort.

Thrashing was essentially costly in fuel and wear. Consequently most enginemen were instinctively opposed to it, but others, not less intelligent, realized that it was very valuable indeed to the railway system to run trains on time even if it did mean thrashing the engine.

CHAPTER EIGHT

CONCLUSION

WORLD WAR II AND AFTER

THE FACT that a good deal of the oil that was regularly imported into Britain just before World War II was dissipated on quite trivial pursuits that could be officially prohibited immediately, gave a fair reserve for purposes related to the war that started in September 1939. Road transport for essential services was not immediately subject to severe restriction on this account, but nevertheless goods traffic on the railways increased and after a year or so rail transport was being pressed to the limit of its resources. Passenger-train services were more and more restricted and the maximum use was being demanded of every class of locomotive in any class of service; streamlined 'Pacifics' could be seen pulling goods trains and (sometimes) twenty-coach passenger trains. Prewar standards of maintenance were, in general, impossible, and engines had so frequently to be allowed to take trains when apparently unfit to do so, that it gradually became learned how badly various classes of locomotive could be neglected before they would not run at all.

In this kind of 'non-stop' service the time and labour required to clean fires and to empty smokeboxes and ashpans became more important than they had been and so more attention was paid in new design to locomotive details designed to minimize the effort required in these operations.

After World War II there were tremendous arrears of maintenance work to be made up on the railways and considerable numbers of locomotives that were better replaced than patched up from their bad conditions. Generous funds were made available and large numbers of new locomotives were built for each of the four groups. There was no pretence of inter-group standardization. Nationalization of the railways had been discussed after World War I and, although it had not been carried out, the grouping of the railways into four units was a step in the direction of unification. So nationalization was also a threat in 1945, and as few could discern any personal profit in it, whatever the overall prospects might be, each group did its best to maintain and to display its individuality in every possible way. Every post-war locomotive design, however numerous its novelties, showed obvious alliances with its predecessors, and every group (except the Great Western) built some of its largest locomotives in numbers that could hardly be justified by traffic expectations but that would add literal weight to its claim for adoption by such locomotive authorities as might be established in a nationalized railway system.

NATIONALIZATION

The four railway groups were combined as a nationalized undertaking known as British Railways on January 1st, 1948. Motive power was in charge of R. A. Riddles, a very well-experienced LMS man and no unbiased observer could have raised objection to that choice. The LMS had been the largest group, since 1932 its locomotive policy had been rational and progressive, and the locomotives added to its stocks during its last sixteen years were as efficient as any similarly aged locomotives in any of the other groups. Given equal personal merit in candidates from all the groups, the size of the LMS was a valid reason for selecting its candidate and the selection committee may well have been glad that such a straightforward discriminant existed. Even the unsuccessful candidates for the top job could hardly complain that they had been unfairly treated. But when Riddles selected his principal

assistants largely from LMS staff this was inevitably regarded
as an example of old-school-tie favouritism. That was not,
in fact, the case; it was simply that, in carrying out what was
clearly going to be a difficult assignment, Riddles needed to
smooth his path in every possible way and one way was to
have next to him technical men with whom he was used
to working and who would not be reluctant to go ahead on
the basis of LMS achievements.

It would, in fact, have been entirely reasonable to adopt
LMS standard designs, as they stood, as British Railways
standard designs. That could well have been a less expensive
way of going about the job than what was actually done.
Perhaps the decision not to use any existing design as a
British Railways standard was merely a means of avoiding
yet another addition to the load of dissatisfaction not un-
naturally felt by non-LMS men whose prospects of promotion
had been reduced by the gigantic merger of nationalization.
Perhaps those LMS men who did not gain by nationalization
felt that the decision to get out entirely new designs was taken
merely as a means of finding a job for the new top men to do.
Any merger of groups of common character is bound to
create unhappiness (for a time at least) in those technical
men who are not industrial politicians, but this was mitigated
in locomotive developments on British Railways by the
decision:

(*a*) to make entirely new designs; and

(*b*) to spread the design work over all the design offices.
No ruthless chief would have complicated the issue by taking
such matters into account, but Riddles accepted human
relations as a vital factor in what was to be done.

By 1948 there were nearly 5,000 diesel-electric locomotives
in main-line service on the American railroads and the
number had been rising by about a thousand a year. For
shunting service, the diesel was well established in many
countries and had a good foothold in Britain. So, after
nationalization, a decision had to be taken as to whether the

future British Railways locomotives were to be diesels but there was no real information about the total cost of running main-line locomotives of that type over any such period as twenty years. The New York Central Railroad had made a detailed analysis in 1946 and the advantage of diesel over steam came out so small as to be within the unavoidable ranges of uncertainties about the figures. (Years later on it was shown that long-term running costs of diesels had been underestimated.) But it was clear that if the motive power on British Railways was to be increased quickly and certainly, the answer was 'steam' and if the maximum amount of new power was to be obtained for any specified expenditure the answer was again 'steam'. In 1948 steam was still the best for British Railways, provided that the locomotives were designed and built to do their work with coal and maintenance much inferior to the standards of 1939.

The nationalized coal of the immediate future demanded in locomotives:

(1) Large grate area for any particular power output, as high combustion rates could not be sustained with poor coal.

(2) Large ashpan volume in relation to grate area to accommodate the higher ash percentages that had to be expected.

Scarcity of labour for shed duties demanded mechanization, so far as possible, of ash disposal and other operations in day-to-day maintenance of locomotives.

Scarcity of enginemen and shed staff demanded easy accessibility of all mechanism and means for quick lubrication without requiring anyone to go under the engine.

It was decided that British Railways locomotives should have:

(1) No crank axle.

(2) No multiple-exhaust arrangement. A properly proportioned plain blast-pipe and chimney could do all that was required at the moderate combustion rates that were postulated.

(3) No exhaust steam injector. Unless maintenance were rigorous, this auxiliary was temperamental and was apt to absorb labour, time, and temper disproportionate to its economy of fuel.

In considering the basis of design for British Railways locomotives it was obviously possible and sensible for the performances and cost-records of the most important existing designs to be examined. Partly as a means of demonstrating that every railway group was being considered, there was an early announcement that a series of locomotive exchanges was to take place in 1948. Locomotives of each group were to be tested with dynamometer cars on regular trains on all the other groups and it was reasonable to expect that this would provide some information about the relative merits of existing designs.

This was very interesting for the locomotive enthusiast and for many of them the subsequent flood of figures about the tests was equally so. The highlight was the evident ability of the LMS 'Rebuilt Scot' 3/4-6-0 to 'pull out' a maximum effort comparable with what could normally be expected of the much larger 'Pacifics'.

The results of the tests were naturally taken into account, along with those of tests made earlier by the various groups, but they were not allowed to affect a decision that no existing design should be adopted as a BR standard. It was also decided that the BR standard designs should have some common external constructional feature that should identify them as 'BR standards'. This was the mounting of a steel sheet, extending over the full width of the locomotive and rising steeply from the level of the buffer beam to that of the running-boards that were set distinctly higher than was necessary to clear the driving wheels. This spoiled the appearance of even the larger designs and the boilers of the smaller ones looked as though they were being throttled. On this dubious score the writer states his own view that the ideal height of the top surface of the running-board is half the height of the

T–F

top of the boiler. Comparison of the LMS class 5 and the LNE class B1 exemplifies this point.

The appearance of the first British Railways standard locomotive was deferred till the occasion of the Festival of Britain at South Bank, London, in 1951. It was a full-size 'Pacific', not quite so large as the largest already running in Britain but unique in having only two cylinders. This was startling as the first British 'Pacific' had four cylinders and the next had three; it seemed inevitable that a locomotive so big as to be a 'Pacific' must have more than two cylinders. The point was, however, that as pre-war operating conditions were unlikely to be reattained, the labour of looking after inside cylinders could not be contemplated and, as pre-war standards of performance were not to be expected, the new 'Pacifics' would not be required to do all that the early ones had done.

The ill-effect of the heavy hammer-blow of the big two-cylinder engines was to be partly offset by a policy of re-laying main lines with flat-bottom rails distinctly heavier and more expensive than the existing standard bull-head rails.

The most unusual visible feature of the 'Britannias' (as these 'Pacifics' were sometimes called after the name of the first one) was the location of the reversing screw close to the reversing shaft instead of in the cab. This was new to Britain but something like it had been done before World War I in a unique 4-4-4 used on the Northern Railway of France. On the 'Britannia' the connexion between the handle shaft and the screw was an inclined shaft provided at each end with a universal joint to accommodate the angle between the shafts. But all three shafts could have been in one line, with no need for any universal joint.

The cab was mounted on the boiler instead of on the frame and this was advantageous in some ways, but the light construction did not make for quietness. The reversing shaft and its attachments were markedly out of rotational balance and large helical springs were afterwards applied to short arms on the shaft in order to diminish the unbalance. Cylinder-cocks controlled by steam instead of rods revived a Belgian practice of the nineteenth century.

The first regular job of the first few 'Britannias' was to run newly accelerated passenger trains between London (Liverpool St) and Ipswich and Norwich. With loads around 300 tons they played with this work and delighted enthusiasts by occasionally touching 90 mph in the dips. It must be added, however, that that speed had been attained on this route at least once (Bib. 25) by a rebuilt GE 4-6-0 of class B12 (R35).

Elsewhere the 'Britannias' had mixed receptions. Some enginemen were put off by their unusual controls (fore-and-aft movement of the regulator handle and fore-and-aft rotation of the reversing handle) and by the noisy riding, but shed staff were delighted with the accessibility of all components that required daily attention.

Some passengers riding in the leading coaches of trains at-attached to 'Britannias' complained about fore-and-aft vibration; firemen found that fire-irons conveniently stowed in a longitudinal compartment on top of the tender were caused by fore-and-aft vibration to work forwards into the cab. Passengers' complaints about longitudinal vibration were eliminated by reducing the preload in the tender drawbar spring so that its elasticity could diminish the vibratory variation in the pull transmitted to the train.

The second BR design to appear in metal, the class 5 2/4-6-0 (R57) was largely a superficially disguised version of the LMS class 5 (R53). The boiler was, in fact, the LMS standard apart from some details but it looked smaller because the running-board was nearly as high as the axis of the smokebox and because the chimney was longer than that fitted to the LMS class 5s after the first batch. In performance these engines were indistinguishable from the LMS class 5 and it may be doubted whether there was any technical justification for building them in preference to an equal number of LMS class 5s.

The 'Clan' class 'Pacific' (R115) was a smaller version of the 'Britannia' but did not perform proportionately to its major dimensions. The particular scope of the 'Clans' was not clearly defined, and they were not brilliant in handling express trains between Lancashire and Glasgow. By the time that this had been established, need for adding to the class was doubtful, and so there was no enthusiasm for the next logical step, which was to subject a 'Clan' to rigorous testing in controlled conditions.

A useful feature (derived from Bulleid) of the BR 'Pacifics' was that each frame-plate was set in the middle of the width of the axleboxes so that the spring hangers could be attached directly to the plates instead of to brackets as was normal practice.

The BR 2/4-6-0s, 2/2-6-0s, and tank engines were, generally speaking, recognizable equivalents of LMS engines, but built up of BR standard components. Noticeably new, however, was the BR 2/2-10-0 (R133) and this turned out to be a more widely useful engine than anyone had expected.

In 1948 the railways of Britain were well supplied with 2/2-8-0 locomotives for goods trains. On the Great Western Railway, for example, the design of 2/2-8-0 introduced in 1903 and subsequently multiplied with only small detail changes to a total of 167, handled all the heavier loose-coupled trains. During World War II, hundreds of 2/2-8-0s had been built, some of LMS design and others of the so-called 'Austerity' design specially contrived so that all the larger locomotive-builders in Great Britain could produce it without difficulty. But the BR policy of planning for poor coal and indifferent maintenance made it necessary to build larger locomotives than 2-8-0s for goods traffic. As a wide firebox was an essential, the obvious wheel arrangement was 2-8-2. But during World War II and afterwards, 'Pacifics' had caused a lot of bother by slipping badly when trying to get big passenger trains on the move. This was partly because indifferent maintenance had made basically indifferent regulators impossible to control with precision, partly because the large volume of big superheaters forbade crisp exclusion of steam from the cylinders and partly because uneven track could allow the bogie and the trailing wheels between them to take a lot of weight off the coupled wheels. Violent slipping of Southern 'Pacifics' and of Thompson 'Pacifics' with quiet exhaust could make one wonder indeed whether the coupled wheels were carrying any weight at all.

Where the distances between successive starts of the train were long, even considerable difficulty in getting the train on the move again might not be very serious, but addiction to slipping could not be tolerated in a goods engine.

So whilst consideration was given to a 2/2-8-2 of 'Britannia' size as a big goods engine, the alternative of a 2/2-10-0 with a wide firebox was also studied. Encouragement of thought in this direction also came from the reflection that the only 2-8-2s ever used in Britain (Gresley designs for the LNE) had not been very successful and from the fact that Riddles had been associated with the design and production of 'Austerity' 2/2-10-0s with wide fireboxes for use in Europe after World War II.

The basic bottleneck in the design of a 2-10-0 for Britain was the restricted space available for the outer parts of the ashpan between the firegrate and the tops of the rear coupled wheels. Because of this, some of the major dimensions of the locomotive depended on the designer's estimate of what is the gentlest side slope of the ashpan 'wings' that will with certainty induce ash to slide down into the middle. What *had* to be done was to set the boiler as high as possible. This feature of the BR 2-10-0s, in conjunction with the clear view through the locomotive between the bottom of the boiler and the tops of the wheels, led to the colloquial application (by some people) of the name 'Space-ships' to these engines.

Some mitigation of the long rigid wheelbase (21 ft 8 ins) was the use of flangeless tyres on the middle pair of coupled wheels. Station-platform clearance by such a long locomotive

made it necessary to set the cylinders so high that they had
to be markedly inclined to the running rails. The provision of
smoke-lifting plates alongside the smokebox suggested that
low exhaust pressure was expected, perhaps in conjunction
with fast running. Omission of steam pipes for coach
heating suggested that the engines were not intended for
passenger-train service.

Nevertheless 2/2-10-0s were, in fact, provided for passenger trains in emergencies when weather did not demand
coach heating, and worked up to speeds that few could have
suspected to be within the ability of a locomotive of this type.
The highest published figure for a BR 2/2-10-0 was 90 mph
corresponding to 8·4 revolutions of the driving wheels per
second, the same as for 6 ft 8 in wheels at 120 mph. When
higher authority became convinced that unofficial reports of
speeds over 70 mph were well founded, speed restriction to
60 mph was imposed on these engines and their use on
passenger trains was discountenanced. Even in ordinary
service, cylinder-wear was unusually rapid and the results
of very fast running would not help to keep the engine out of
the repair shops.

Apart from objections on this score, the BR 2/2-10-0 was
surely the supreme mixed-traffic engine ever to run in
Britain. With moderate axle loading, plenty of power from a
40 sq ft grate, high tractive effort possible with 78-ton
adhesion weight (and no rear truck to detract from it), and
ability to run fast, it could do any job reasonably well and
most jobs better than any other British locomotive could do
them. It was appropriate that the last steam locomotive to be
built by BR was a 2/2-10-0 and Swindon Works emphasized
the situation by applying to the double chimney a copper rim
and by adding to the smoke-lifting plates (the running-board
valances would have been better sites) the name *Evening
Star* in the superb Victorian typeface used almost exclusively
by the Great Western for engines' names after the death of
Queen Victoria.

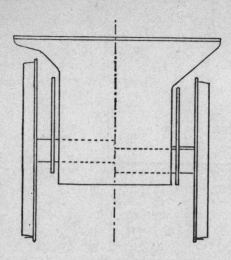

13. Cross-sections of ashpans over coupled wheels.
5 ft wheel on left; 4 ft 6 in wheel on right

Had the designer of the class 9 foreseen its speed with 5-ft wheels, he might have used 4 ft 6 in wheels instead, and comparison of the right-hand and left-hand parts of Fig 13, above, shows that this would have admitted an ashpan with non-choking wings, eliminating a weak point in the class 9 design. Right to the very end of steam, designers were under-estimating the menace of the ashpan!

The Franco-Crosti system (Fig 14, p 156) for heating feed-water by smokebox gases was embodied in a number of 2/2-10-0s built with boilers specially designed for the purpose but it failed to justify itself. Sulphur dioxide in gases cooled by the secondary tubes (2) attacked them just as it attacks the upper parts of domestic chimneys unprotected by soot (Bib. 37, p 139).

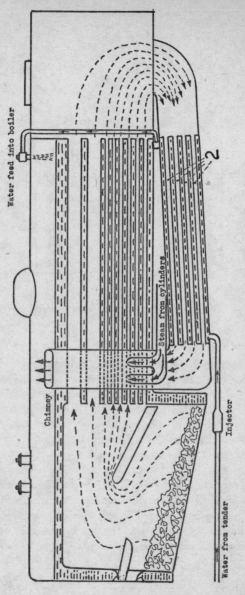

Water feed into boiler

Chimney

Steam from cylinders

2

Injector

Water from tender

14. Franco-Crosti boiler (diagrammatic)

GENERAL

Although an immense amount of information about design and performance of major and minor components of British locomotives was studied in preparing the B R standard designs, and although the indisputably expert officials responsible for them were on their mettle to avoid any ground for criticism of them by the other technical experts of the four former railway groups, defects nevertheless showed up.

Although the boilers of the 'Britannias' were originally fitted with steam collectors specially intended to minimize the possibility of picking up water besides steam, this happened soon after 'Britannias' went into service and cylinder-ends were knocked out and pistons broken by trapped water.

Later on, coupling-rods were broken when driving wheels slipped at high running speeds. In this condition resonant rotational vibration (Bib. 32) of coupled wheels and coupling-rods could produce so great a compressive load in a rod as to cause it to fail by bending horizontally away from the wheels. This it did because its I-section was very weak in that direction. The operation of forming the I-section by milling away material from a rectangular slab threw away 80 per cent of its strength in this direction. The remedy was to omit the milling operation and to use the rectangular section. The Great Western had found this out in 1906.

Slide-bars in 'Britannias' were attached in a way that made it difficult to tighten the securing nuts properly. This was altered after loss of a bottom slide-bar from a 'Britannia' led to failure of the piston rod and connecting-rod, which fell and deformed the adjacent track at just the moment that caused a train on it to be derailed into the coaches behind the 'Britannia' (Settle, January 21st, 1960, Bib. 33).

Less drastic, but very disappointing after the comfort of the enginemen had been specially considered in laying out the controls in the cab, was the circumstance that the noise in the cabs (at least those of tender engines) was much worse than in the average British cab in use before nationalization.

The fact that the most expertly designed British steam locomotives could have imperfections means only that it is hard to think of everything. It tends to extenuate the mistakes made now and again by all designers of locomotives and of everything else.

FOREIGN FLYER

There is enough of interest in British locomotive history to fill many books of this size, but nevertheless the author cannot refrain from looking at one superlative class of locomotive that never ran in Britain although one at least of its members came as close as Calais. This was a design of four-cylinder compound, produced by extensive rebuilding of a 4C/4-6-2 of the Paris–Orleans Railway by Monsieur A. Chapelon to the rare 4-8-0 wheel arrangement, in order to provide reliable motive power for heavy passenger trains over the steeply graded route from Vierzon to Toulouse. For power in relation to size, for high thermal efficiency at high power and for sure-footedness in heavy pulling, this design left the rest of the world well behind. Students of the locomotive, professional and amateur alike, read reports of their doings with incredulous amazement. Performance was rigorously and exhaustively tested and the full story is given in a book written by Chapelon and published by Dunod (Paris) in 1935. A locomotive of about the same size as a Gresley 'Pacific' could beat its power output by 50 per cent at any speed and could do it on less coal per unit of useful work done. That was the position in 1934 although, by 1940, a Gresley A4 with double chimney on one special occasion (see Appendix 3) substantially reduced the difference in power-for-size.

The Chapelon 4-8-0 was too wide (9ft 10 ins) to run in

Britain but many people wondered how to design a British locomotive to approximate to its level of performance. A careful analysis (Bib. 29) showed that the 4-8-0's distinction arose, not from compounding, high superheat or poppet valves but from its feed-water heater, its double chimney, its appropriately high nominal tractive effort and the remarkably high efficiency of its boiler at high combustion rates. For this last item the thermic syphon and the Serve (internally ribbed) tubes were probably responsible.

The biggest efforts of the Chapelon 4-8-0s (up to 2,400 dhp continuously and Grade 29 in the scheme of Appendix 3) made hard work for the fireman if sustained for more than an hour or two. To avoid this, mechanical stokers were later applied to some of these engines, but nothing was published in Britain about consumption of coal fed to them by that means.

The Chapelon 4-8-0 was a four-cylinder compound of the traditional French type and, even with the largest cylinders that could be accommodated within the loading gauge, the need for a nominal tractive effort of about 56,000 lb forced the designer up to a boiler pressure of 290 psi which demanded a heavy boiler and involved high maintenance cost by British standards.

When making its maximum efforts the engine worked at expansion ratios well within the economic range of single expansion. Adoption of that principle in a new design would make it possible to keep down the boiler pressure to 200 psi without detriment to anything and with great advantage to the boiler. Moreover, such a locomotive could be made narrow enough to run in Britain.

Four piston valves worked by two Walschaerts valve gears and two rocking levers were far less complicated than the sixteen poppet valves, four Walschaerts valve gears, rocking shafts, and camshafts of the French engine and were very much more readily accessible. The feed-water heater might justify retention although there would be insufficient room for it on top of a 6-ft. boiler under the British loading gauge.

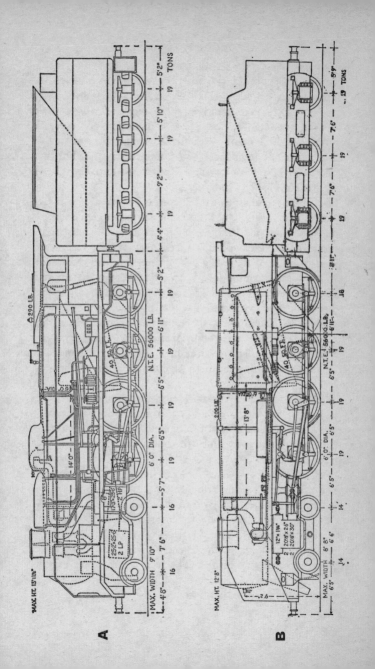

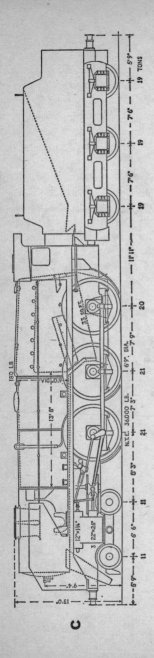

C

A Chapelon 4C/4-8-0

B Possible equivalent 4/4-8-0 within British limits

C Compromise between Derby proposal (1924) and R62

A four-cylinder simple equivalent of the Chapelon 4-8-0 might have been fitted into the British loading gauge and Fig B (p 160) shows how it might have looked. It has about the largest inside cylinders that could be placed over the bogie with room for adequate axleboxes on the leading coupled axle. The outside cylinders drive the second coupled axle so that the connecting-rods can be long enough to permit 30-in piston stroke.

The special characteristics of such a locomotive would have been most valuable on such hilly routes as Leeds–Carlisle–Edinburgh–Aberdeen but it might also have equalled its French progenitor in ability to equal the booked times of the British pre-1940 streamlined trains with twice their normal loads.

The inevitably severe wear and tear of a locomotive working continuously at the Chapelon limit would have prohibited such working as a regular practice in Britain, but an engine able to 'pull out' an extra 50 per cent in emergency could render incalculable benefit in bringing a delayed main-line train back on to schedule.

BRITISH RAILWAYS, GROUPED AND PRE-GROUPED

CHIEF BRITISH RAILWAYS FROM 1900

THE FOLLOWING information is limited to railways with more than 300 locomotives at the end of 1922.

For each railway is given the official name, the location of the main locomotive works, and the number of locomotives owned by the company at the end of 1922.

Then follow the names of the locomotive superintendents (or chief mechanical engineers) over the period 1900 to 1923.

Similar information is given in respect of each of the four groups formed in 1923.

LONDON MIDLAND & SCOTTISH RAILWAY GROUP (LMS)

	Works	*Locomotives*
London & North Western	Crewe	3,469
1871–1903 F. W. Webb		
1903–1909 G. Whale		
1909–1920 C. J. Bowen-Cooke		
1920–1921 H. P. M. Beames		
1921–1923 G. Hughes		
Midland	Derby	3,019
1873–1903 S. W. Johnson		
1903–1909 R. M. Deeley		
1909–1923 H. Fowler		
Lancashire & Yorkshire	Horwich (Nr Bolton)	1,654

1899–1904   H. A. Hoy
1904–1922   G. Hughes

| Caledonian | St Rollox (Glasgow) | 1,077 |

1895–1914   J. F. McIntosh
1914–1923   W. Pickersgill

| Glasgow & South Western | Kilmarnock | 528 |

1890–1912   J. Manson
1912–1918   P. Drummond
1918–1923   R. H. Whitelegg

LMS *group*   10,402 locomotives
1922–1925   G. Hughes
1925–1931   Sir Henry Fowler
1931–1932   E. H. J. Lemon
1932–1944   W. A. Stanier
1944–1945   C. E. Fairburn
1945–1948   H. G. Ivatt

LONDON & NORTH EASTERN RAILWAY GROUP (LNE)

	Works	*Locomotives*
North Eastern	Darlington	2,143

1890–1910   W. Worsdell
1910–1923   Sir Vincent Raven

| Great Northern | Doncaster | 1,359 |

1896–1911   H. A. Ivatt
1911–1923   H. N. Gresley

| Great Central | Gorton (Manchester) | 1,358 |

1900–1923   J. G. Robinson

| Great Eastern | Stratford (London) | 1,330 |

1885–1907   J. Holden
1907–1912   S. D. Holden
1912–1923   A. J. Hill

North British	Cowlairs (Glasgow)	1,074

1882–1903   M. Holmes
1903–1919   W. P. Reid
1919–1923   W. Chalmers

LNE *group*   7,392 locomotives
1923–1941   H. N. Gresley
1941–1946   E. Thompson
1946–1948   A. H. Peppercorn

GREAT WESTERN RAILWAY GROUP

	Works	*Locomotives*
Great Western	Swindon	3,251

1877–1902   W. Dean
1902–1922   G. J. Churchward

GW *group*   4,050 locomotives
1923–1941   C. B. Collett
1941–1948   F. W. Hawksworth

SOUTHERN RAILWAY GROUP (SR)

	Works	*Locomotives*
London & South Western	Eastleigh	915

1895–1912   D. Drummond
1912–1923   R. W. Urie

South Eastern & Chatham	Ashford	729

1898–1913   H. S. Wainwright
1913–1923   R. E. L. Maunsell

London Brighton & South Coast   Brighton   619
1890–1905   R. J. Billinton
1905–1911   D. Earle Marsh
1911–1923   L. B. Billinton

SR *group*   2,285 locomotives
1923–1937   R. E. L. Maunsell
1937–1948   O. V. S. Bulleid

DIMENSIONS OF LOCOMOTIVES

MAJOR DIMENSIONS of certain classes of British steam locomotives are tabulated below. Reasonable limitation of space prohibits the display of every dimension that any reader might like to have. The restricted list used in Appendix 2 aims to indicate limitations imposed on the power of the locomotive.

Notation

d = diameter of cylinders (ins)

D = diameter of driving wheels (ins)

G = grate area (sq ft)

H = (heating surface of superheater)/grate area

L = lap of valves (ins)

s = stroke of pistons (ins)

S_c = (50 to 70)G/t for superheated steam
or (42 to 58)G/t for saturated steam

S_v = (330 to 660)DVL/d^2s for piston valves and super-heated steam
Multiply by 0·86 for saturated steam or use
(90 to 180)D/ds for flat valves and saturated steam

p = maximum boiler pressure (psi)

t = nominal tractive effort (1,000 lb)

V = diameter of piston valves (ins)

Grate Area (G)

This imposes an upper limit on the sustained power at any particular combustion rate.

Nominal Tractive Effort $(t) = (0·425pd^2s/1000D) \times$ No of cylinders (LP only, in a compound)

This is the mean value (during any revolution of the driving wheel) of the backward push that the locomotive could exert on the rails when in full gear with maximum boiler pressure if the friction between coupled wheels and rails were great enough to transmit that pull and if there were no friction anywhere else.

Elasticity and slackness in the draw-gear make it possible for the momentary maximum drawbar-pull on starting to exceed the nominal tractive effort by anything up to 30 per cent.

The figure quoted in Appendix 2 for nominal tractive effort is the number of thousands of pounds above that calculated in the ordinary way for mean effective pressure equal to 0·85 times the maximum boiler pressure. (Re-boring of cylinders and re-turning of tyres of coupled wheels both increase the nominal tractive effort.)

Diameter of cylinders (d), stroke of pistons (s), diameter of coupled wheels (D)

These are traditionally quoted and are used in calculating nominal tractive effort and best speed-ranges.

Weights

Adhesion weight (ie, weight on coupled wheels) sets a limit to the sustained pull of the locomotive.

Total weight (in conjunction with wheelbase) limits the routes on which a locomotive may run.

Actual weights could exceed published figures by anything up to 5 per cent.

On each figure there is an uncertainty of at least a ton each way.

Superheat

The ratio of heating surface of superheater to area of grate is an approximate indication of the degree of superheating intended by the designer.

Speed-ranges

S_v is the speed-range to which highest cylinder efficiency is limited by dimensions of valves.

S_c is the speed-range to which highest cylinder efficiency is limited by nominal tractive effort when the indicated horse-power (ihp) is 45 times the grate area. (The figure 45 is arbitrarily chosen; it represents a pretty brisk sustained combustion rate but many locomotives could work much harder than this.)

The overlap of S_v and S_c is the speed-range over which the highest practicable cylinder efficiency is possible.

For many classes of locomotive (for nearly all of those with flat valves) there was no such overlap and so they could never achieve the highest efficiency that might have been attained if the designer had sought it.

Where, as for example R65, the S_v range is above the S_c range, the locomotive would have a wider speed-range at highest efficiency when worked harder than 45 ihp per sq ft of grate area.

Valves and Valve gear (in the column headed Y)

F implies flat valves

P implies piston valves

Letters J, S, and W imply valve gear of Joy, Stephenson, or Walschaerts type.

Notes

1. Many locomotives built with flat valves and no super-heater were later rebuilt with piston valves and superheaters. The figures quoted relate (in general) to the condition in which the class did its most important work.

2. Speed-range S_v is calculated for clean valves of the dimensions published or derivable from published ones. Carbonization of valves could invalidate the figures by altering effective lap and lead.

3. Following an entry in column G:

    A implies double chimney with plain blast-pipes

    K implies Kylchap double chimney

    L implies Lemaître multiple exhaust.

4. The entry 'No in class' gives an idea of the numerical size of the class. It is not claimed that any entry in this column is correct to the last digit.

Ref	Rly	G Grate Area (sq ft)	D Wheel Dia ft	D Wheel Dia ins	d Cyl Dia ins	s Piston stroke ins	t Nom TE (1,000 lb)	Wt Ad tons	Wt Tot tons
1	GW	17·4	5	2	17½	24	20	44	44
2	MR	21·1	5	3	20	26	25	49	49
3	GN	19	5	2	19	26	21	53	53
4	GC	19·5	5	2	18½	26	22	53	53
5	NE	20	4	8	18½	26	25	49	49
6	GE	26·5	4	11	20	28	29	55	55
7	LNE	26	5	2	20	26	26	58	58
8	SR	27L	5	1	19	26	30	52	52
9	GW	20·4	5	8	18	26	21	34	52
10	GW	17·2	5	8	18	26	19	31	49
11	LNW	22·4	6	9	19	26	18	38	59
12	LNW	22·4	6	9	20½	26	20	39	60
13	MR	28·4	6	6	19	26	22	37	58
14	GN	19	6	8	18½	26	16	36	54
15	GC	26·5	6	9	20	26	20	42	61
16	NE	27	6	10	19	26	22	42	60
17	LY	18·8	7	3	20	26	19	33	48
18	GE	21·3	7	0	19	26	17	35	52
19	LSW	27	6	7	19½	26	20	40	62
20	LBS	24	6	9	19	26	18	36	49
21	SE	24	6	6	19	26	19	34	53
22	CR	21	6	6	20	26	19	38	59
23	NB	21	6	6	19	26	20	37	55
24	GSW	24·8	6	7	20	26	18	37	59
25	GW	20·6	6	8½	18	30	21	38	59
26	MR	28·4	6	9	19/21	26	24	39	62
27	LNE	26	6	8	17	26	22	42	66
28	SR	28·3	6	7	16½	26	25	42	67
29	LNW	25	6	3	19	26	19	45	64
30	LNW	25	5	3	19	26	22	44	63
31	LNW	25	6	3	20½	26	22	47	66

H Super Grate	S_v mph	S_c mph	Y	Date of first	No in class	Class
0-6-0						
4·2	14–28	36–51	FS	1930	120	2251
12·0	18–36	42–59	PS	1911	762	4F
14·3	22–44	45–63	PS	1911	110	J22 LNE J6
—	12–24	37–52	FS	1901	174	973 LNE J11
—	11–22	34–47	FS	1906	130	P3 LNE J27
7·6	21–42	46–64	PS	1920	25	1270 LNE J20
10·4	20–40	50–70	PS	1926	280	J39
8·1	35–70	45–63	PS	1942	40	Q1
4-4-0						
4·0	24–48	48–68	PS	1908	15	Bird (Double fr)
4·7	24–48	45–63	PS	1936	20	3200 (Double fr)
—	15–30	51–72	FJ	1904	130	Precursor
13·4	30–60	56–78	PJ	1910	90	George
—	14–28	54–75	PW	1907	10	999
14·3	30–60	60–83	PS	1911	15	D1 LNE D1
11·4	31–62	66–92	PS	1913	45	Director LNE D10/11
—	15–30	51–71	PS	1908	10	R1 LNE D21
13·8	31–62	49–69	PW	1908	4	1098
—	15–30	53–73	FS	1900	111	S46
9·3	24–48	67–84	PW	1912	10	463
—	15–30	56–77	FS	1899	33	B4
9·5	45–90	63–88	PS	1919	32	E1 Rebuilt
15·7	22–44	55–77	PS	1910	22	139
—	14–28	44–61	FS	1909	43	Scott LNE D30
13·5	25–50	69–96	PS	1913	1	341
2/4-4-0						
9·3	45–90	50–70	PS	1904	40	County
3/4-4-0						
10·3	16–32	59–83	PS/FS	1903	245	Compound
10·5	42–84	59–83	PW	1927	75	D49
10	47–94	57–79	PW	1930	40	School
4-6-0						
—	15–30	55–77	FJ	1905	105	Experiment
—	12–24	47–67	FJ	1906	170	19 in goods
12	28–56	57–80	PJ	1911	245	Prince

Ref	Rly	G Grate Area (sq ft)	D Wheel Dia ft	ins	d Cyl Dia ins	s Piston stroke ins	t Nom TE (1,000 lb)	Wt Ad tons	Tot
32	GC	26	6	9	21½	26	23	58	76
33	GC	26	5	7	21½	26	28	57	75
34	GE	26·5	6	6	20	28	22	44	63
35	LNE	31	6	6	20	28	22	48	70
36	CR	26	6	6	21	26	22	55	73
37	GW	27·1	6	8½	18½	30	25	55	72
38	GW	27·1	6	0	18½	30	28	56	75
39	GW	27·1	5	8	18½	30	29	55	74
40	GW	22·1	5	8	18	30	27	51	69
41	GW	28·8	6	3	18½	30	33	59	77
42	GC	23·5	5	3	19	26	20	50	65
43	GC	26·3	6	7	19	26	19	55	71
44	GC	23·5	5	4	19½	26	23	52	67
45	GC	26·0	5	8	21	26	26	54	73
46	NE	27·0	5	8	18½	26	30	59	78
47	LSW	30	6	0	21	28	27	61	82
48	LSW	30	6	7	22	28	27	56	78
49	CR	25·5	6	1	20	28	23	56	75
50	HR	26	5	9	19½	26	22	44	60
51	HR	26	6	0	21	26	23	52	68
52	GSW	28	5	8½	19½	28	24	56	75
53	LMS	28·7	6	0	18½	28	26	54	71
54	LNE	27·5	6	2	20	26	27	53	71
55	SR	30	6	7	20½	28	26	60	81
56	SR	28	5	7	20½	28	30	60	81
57	BR	28·7	6	2	19	28	26	58	76
58	BR	26·7	5	8	18	28	26	52	68
59	LMS	31·2	6	9	18	26	34	63	85
60	LMS	30·5	6	9	18	26	27	60	81
61	LMS	31	6	9	17	26	27	60	80
62	LMS	31A	6	9	18	26	34	60	82
63	LNE	27·5	6	8	17½	26	26	55	78
64	LNE	27	5	8	18½	26	30	59	79

H Super Grate	S_v mph	S_c mph	Y	Date of first	No in class	Class
16·5	22–44	57–80	PS	1912	6	Sir Sam Fay LNE B2
16·5	18–36	46–65	PS	1913	11	Glenalmond LNE B8
10·8	27–54	60–84	PS	1911	80	1500 LNE B12
10·2	33–66	35–50	PS	1932	52	R34 rebuilt
19·8	23–46	59–83	PS	1906	5	Cardean

2/4-6-0

9·6	42–84	54–76	PS	1903	77	Saint
9·6	37–74	48–68	PS	1925	330	Hall
9·6	36–72	46–75	PS	1936	80	Grange
7·2	37–74	41–57	PS	1938	30	Manor
8·8	39–78	36–50	PS	1945	30	County
—	12–24	50–68	FS	1902	14	1067 LNE B5
—	15–30	58–80	FS	1906	10	1095 LNE B4
—	11–22	43–60	FS	1906	10	1105 LNE B9
11·8	20–40	50–70	PS	1918	3	416 LNE B6
14·8	22–44	45–63	PS	1911	38	S2 LNE B15
11	21–42	56–77	PW	1913	10	H15 '482'
10·2	21–42	56–77	PW	1918	20	N15 '736'
10·1	23–46	55–77	PS	1916	26	60
—	12–24	50–68	FS	1900	19	Castle
15·8	26–52	56–79	PS	1919	8	Clan
15·7	32–64	58–81	PW	1924	5	500
10·7	37–74	55–77	PW	1934	840	5
12·5	38–76	51–71	PW	1942	440	B1(1942)
11·2	33–66	58–81	PW	1925	54	King Arthur
12	28–56	47–66	PW	1927	25	S15
12·8	45–90	52–73	PW	1951	172	5
10	42–84	52–73	PW	1951	80	4

3/4-6-0

9·7	41–82	46–64	PW	1927	71	Royal Scot
12	41–82	56–79	PW	1930	52	Baby Scot
10	52–104	57–80	PW	1935	190	Silver Jubilee
11·4	41–82	46–64	PW	1943	70	Rebuilt Scot
12·5	43–86	51–71	PW	1928	73	B17
16	34–68	45–63	PW	1937	22	Rebuilt B16

Ref	Rly	G Grate Area (sq ft)	D Wheel Dia ft	ins	d Cyl Dia ins	s Piston stroke ins	t Nom TE (1,000 lb)	Wt Ad tons	Tot
65	GW	27·1	6	8½	15	26	28	56	76
66	GW	29·4	6	8½	16	26	32	59	8o
67	GW	34·3	6	6	16	28	40	68	9o
68	LNW	30·5	6	9	16	26	25	59	78
69	GC	26·0	6	9	16	26	25	57	79
70	GC	26·0	5	8	16	26	30	59	8o
71	LY	27	6	3	16	26	27	59	77
72	LY	27	6	3	16½	26	29	59	79
73	LSW	31·5	6	7	15	26	22	55	77
74	GSW	28	6	7	14	26	20	51	71
75	SR	33	6	7	16½	26	34	62	84
76	GW	20·6	5	8	18½	30	26	52	62
77	GN	24	5	8	20	26	23	52	62
78	GN	24	5	8	20	26	23	54	64
79	LBS	24·8	5	6	21	26	25	53	64
80	SEC	25·0	5	6	19	28	26	53	62
81	SEC	25·0	6	0	19	28	24	53	62
82	LMS	27·5	5	6	21	26	27	57	67
83	GN	28·0	5	8	18½	26	30	61	73
84	SR	25·0	5	6	16	28	28	54	64
85	SR	25·0	6	0	16	28	26	54	64
86	LNW	23·6	4	5	19½	24	26	59	59
87	LNW	23·6	4	5	20½	24	28	62	62
88	GN	24·5	4	8	20	26	28	55	55
89	HB	22	4	6	19	26	30	62	62
90	LY	23	4	6	20	26	30	57	57
91	LY	25·6	4	6	21½	26	34	67	67
92	CR	23	4	6	21	26	32	61	61
93	LMS	23·6	4	8½	19	26	30	61	61
94	GC	23·5	4	8	19	26	26	62	62
95	NE	21·5	4	7	20	26	29	59	59
96	NE	23	4	7	20	26	26	63	63

H Super Grate	S_v mph	S_c mph	Y	Date of first	No in class	Class
4/4-6-0						
9·6	58–116	48–68	PW	1907	73	Star
8·9	52–104	46–64	PW	1923	170	Castle
9·1	54–108	43–60	PW	1927	30	King
13·6	40–80	61–85	PW	1913	130	Claughton
13·2	32–64	52–73	PS	1917	6	1169 LNE B3
13·2	27–54	43–60	PS	1921	38	72 LNE B7
—	16–33	50–70	PJ	1908	20	1500
14·6	38–76	47–65	PW	1921	20	Reb 1500
8·5	40–80	71–100	PW	1911	10	T14 443
15·7	61–122	70–98	PW	1915	10	400
11·4	47–94	48–68	PW	1926	16	Lord Nelson
2/2-6-0						
9·3	36–72	40–56	PS	1911	342	4300
12·4	25–50	52–73	PW	1912	10	1630 LNE K1
16·4	25–50	52–73	PW	1913	65	1640 LNE K2
11·2	23–46	50–70	PS	1913	17	337
11·4	34–68	48–67	PW	1917	80	N
11·4	37–74	52–73	PW	1928	60	U
11·2	34–68	51–71	PW	1927	245	Horwich
3/2-6-0						
15·0	30–60	45–63	PW	1920	193	1000 LNE K3
11·4	49–98	45–63	PW	1923	3	N1
11·4	53–106	48–67	PW	1928	21	U1
0-8-0						
—	10–20	38–53	FJ	1906	63	D
16	16–32	42–59	PJ	1912	170	G1
—	10–20	37–51	FS	1901	55	401 LNE Q1
—	10–20	31–43	FS	1907	15	LNE Q10
—	9–18	32–44	FJ	1900	110	No 500
13·3	17–34	38–53	PJ	1910	120	No 9
—	9–18	30–42	FS	1901	8	600
15	35–70	39–55	PW	1929	25	Fowler
2/0-8-0						
—	10–20	38–53	FS	1902	89	1052 LNE Q4
—	13–26	31–43	PS	1901	90	T1 LNE Q5
19	15–30	46–64	PS	1913	120	T2 LNE Q6

Ref	Rly	G Grate Area (sq ft)	D Wheel Dia ft ins		d Cyl Dia ins	s Piston stroke ins	t Nom TE (1,000 lb)	Wt Ad tons	Tot
97	NE	27	4	7	18½	26	38	72	72
98	GW	27·1	4	7½	18½	30	35	67	76
99	GW	30·3	5	8	19	30	31	73	82
100	GN	27	4	8	21	28	32	67	76
101	GC	26·3	4	8	21	26	32	66	73
102	LMS	28·7	4	8½	18½	28	33	62	71
103	LNE	27·9	4	8	20	26	36	66	73
104	GN	27·5	4	8	18½	26	37	70	79
105	LY	26	7	3	19	26	17	35	59
106	GW	27·1	6	8½	18	30	23	40	72
107	GN	31	6	8	20	24	18	40	70
108	GC	26·3	6	9	19	26	18	37	72
109	NE	27	6	10	19½	28	20	40	74
110	LBS	31	6	8	21	26	21	38	69
111	NB	28·5	6	9	20	28	24	40	75
112	NE	27	6	10	16½	26	20	41	79
113	GC	26·3	6	9	19/21	26	24	37	74
114	BR	42	6	2	20	28	32	62	94
115	BR	36	6	2	19½	28	28	57	89
116	GN	41·3	6	8	20	26	30	60	92
117	NE	41·5	6	8	19	26	30	60	97
118	LNE	41·3	6	8	19	26	33	66	96
119	LNE	41·3	6	8	18½	26	36	66	103

H Super Grate	S_v mph	S_c mph	Y	Date of first	No in class	Class
3/0-8-0						
19·6	18–36	35–50	PS	1919	15	T3 LNE Q7
2/2-8-0						
9·6	28–56	38–54	PS	1903	167	2800
9·6	35–70	49–68	PS	1919	9	4700
21·1	18–36	42–59	PW	1913	20	456
9·2	16–32	41–48	PS	1911	129	966 LNE O4
7·5	29–58	43–61	PW	1935	630	8F
12·3	29–58	39–54	PW	1944	58	Rebuilt O4
3/2-8-0						
15·7	25–50	38–52	PW	1918	11	O2 LNE O2
4-4-2						
—	16–32	64–89	FJ	1899	40	1400
2/4-4-2						
9·6	44–88	59–82	PS	1904	13	172
18·3	42–84	86–120	PS	1902	94	251 LNE C1
9·2	25–50	61–86	PS	1903	27	192 LNE C4
—	23–46	57–78	PS	1903	20	V1 LNE C6
14·9	23–46	74–103	PS	1905	11	H1/2
—	21–42	50–69	PS	1906	22	I & H LNE C10
3/4-4-2						
16·0	42–84	67–94	PS	1911	50	Z LNE C7
3C/4-4-s						
—	13–26	42–58	PS/FS	1905	4	258 LNE C5
2/4-6-2						
17	40–80	66–92	PW	1951	55	7 Britannia
17·5	43–86	64–90	PW	1951	10	6 Clan
3/4-6-2						
12·8	25–50	69–96	PW	1922	52	A1 LNE A1
16·7	25–50	69–96	PS	1922	5	2400 LNE **A2**
15·3	37–74	62–87	PW	1928	27	A3
18·2	43–86	57–80	PW	1935	35	A4

Ref	Rly	G Grate Area (sq ft)	D Wheel Dia ft	D Wheel Dia ins	d Cyl Dia ins	s Piston stroke ins	t Nom TE (1,000 lb)	Wt Ad tons	Wt Tot tons
120	LNE	50	6	2	19	26	41	66	101
121	LNE	41K	6	2	19	26	37	66	98
122	LNE	50K	6	2	19	26	41	66	103
123	LNE	50K	6	8	19	26	38	66	104
124	SR	48L	6	2	18	24	38	65	98
125	SR	38L	6	2	16½	24	31	58	90
126	GW	41·8	6	8½	15	26	28	60	98
127	LMS	45	6	6	16	28	40	68	105
128	LMS	50	6	9	16½	28	40	67	105
129	LNE	41·3	6	2	18½	26	34	66	93
130	LNE	28·5	5	8	15	26	28	49	71
131	LNE	41·3	5	2	20	26	39	72	100
132	LNE	50	6	2	21	26	44	81	110
133	BR	40·2	5	0	20	28	40	78	87
134	MR	31·5	4	7½	16·8	28	44	74	74
135	GW	15·3	4	7½	17½	24	23	49	49
136	GW	17·4	4	7½	17½	24	23	55	55
137	GN	16·3	4	8	18½	26	24	58	58
138	GE	14·5	4	0	16½	22	19	43	43
139	LBS	17·4	4	6	17½	26	22	54	54
140	LMS	16	4	7	18	26	21	50	50
141	LNW	17	5	2	18	24	17	42	52
142	GW	20·4	4	7½	18	26	26	56	69
143	GN	19	5	8	18	26	18	52	66
144	GN	19	5	8	19	26	20	55	72
145	GE	17·7	4	10	18	24	21	49	62

H Super Grate	S_v mph	S_c mph	Y	Date of first	No in class	Class
13·6	42–84	61–85	PW	1947	25	A2 Peppercorn
16·5	42–84	56–78	PW	1944	4	A2/1 Thompson
13·6	42–84	61–85	PW	1946	15	A2/3 Thompson
13·6	46–92	66–92	PW	1948	40	A1 Peppercorn
12·6	55–110	64–89	PW	1941	30	Merchant Navy
12·7	50–100	62–86	PW	1945	118	West Country
4/4-6-2						
13	58–116	75–105	PW	1908	1	111 *The Great Bear*
13·8	60–120	56–78	PW	1933	12	Princess
17·2	55–110	62–87	PW	1938	38	Duchess
3/2-6-2						
16·2	40–80	61–85	PW	1936	184	V2
12·5	38–76	51–71	PW	1941	2	V4
3/2-8-2						
12·7	20–40	53–74	PW	1925	2	P1
12·7	31–62	57–80	PW	1934	6	P2
2/2-10-0						
13·2	33–66	50–70	PW	1954	251	9
4/0-10-0						
14	10–20	36–50	PW	1920	1	2290
0-6-0T						
—	12–24	28–39	FS	1929	863	5700 PT
4·3	13–26	38–53	FS	1947	210	9400 PT
—	10–20	28–39	FS	1913	40	Ardsley LNE J50
—	12–24	38–53	FS	1902	89	S56 LNE J69
—	11–22	33–46	FS	1913	10	E2
—	11–22	32–44	FS	1924	422	3F
0-6-2T						
—	13–26	42–58	FJ	1881	300	18 in tank
4·0	19–38	36–50	PS	1924	200	5600
—	13–26	33–46	FS	1906	54	1560 LNE N1
10·9	24–48	48–67	PS	1920	60	1721 N2
5·8	27–54	42–59	PW	1915	62	1000 LNE N7

T–G

Ref	Rly	G Grate Area (sq ft)	D Wheel Dia ft ins		d Cyl Dia ins	s Piston stroke ins	t Nom TE (1,000 lb)	Wt Ad tons	Tot
146	LSW	20·4	5	7	18½	26	20	36	60
147	LMS	17·5	5	7	18	26	17	34	58
148	GW	20·4	5	2	17	24	18	35	65
149	LY	18·8	5	8	20½	26	25	40	67
150	LNW	22·4	6	3	19	26	19	40	75
151	GN	17·8	5	7	17½	26	18	34	60
152	GC	19·6	5	7	19	26	17	37	67
153	LBS	23·7	6	9	19	26	18	38	76
154	NB	16·6	5	4	19	26	21	38	74
155	GW	20·4	6	8½	18	30	21	37	75
156	LTS	19·8	6	6	19	26	18	37	72
157	GW	16·6	5	2	17½	24	21	49	62
158	LY	26	5	8	19	26	22	53	78
159	GW	16·6	4	7½	17	24	25	46	61
160	GW	20·6	5	8	18½	30	26	58	82
161	GW	20·4	5	8	18	30	25/28	53	79
162	LMS	17·5	5	3	17½	26	22	47	72
163	LMS	19·2	5	3	17½	26	22	47	72
164	BR	17·5	5	0	16½	24	19	39	63
165	LNE	22	5	8	16	26	23	57	84
166	GC	26·5	5	11	21	26	29	60	98

H Super Grate	S_v mph	S_c mph	Y	Date of first	No in class	Class
0-4-4T						
—	13–26	42–59	FS	1897	105	M7
—	13–26	43–60	FS	1932	10	Stanier
2-4-2T						
—	14–28	57–80	FS	1900	31	3600
9·1	21–42	38–53	PJ	1911	20	227 No. 18
4-4-2T						
—	14–28	50–69	FJ	1906	50	Precursor Tank
—	13–26	42–58	FS	1898	60	C12 LNE C12
—	12–24	48–67	FS	1903	52	1055 LNE C13/4
10·7	28–56	66–92	PS	1908	27	I3
13·3	20–40	33–46	PS	1911	51	L/M LNE C15/16
2/4-4-2T						
4	41–82	45–62	PS	1905	50	County Tank
—	14–28	46–64	FS	1909	35	79
2-6-2T						
6·2	13–26	33–46	FS	1907	20	Reb 0-6-0
—	12–24	50–70	FJ	1903	20	Hoy
2/2-6-2T						
4·7	33–66	30–43	PS	1906	175	4500
9·3	36–72	40–55	PS	1906	41	3150
4·0	38–76	35–49	PS	1929	250	5100/6100
9·9	26–52	40–56	PW	1930	70	Fowler
4·2	42–84	40–56	PW	1935	139	Stanier
7·7	31–62	46–64	PW	1963	30	2
3/2-6-2T						
13	43–86	48–67	PW	1930	92	V1 V3
2-6-4T						
11·6	18–36	46–64	PS	1914	20	272

Ref	Rly	G Grate Area (sq ft)	D Wheel Dia ft ins		d Cyl Dia ins	s Piston stroke ins	t Nom TE (1,000 lb)	Wt Ad tons	Tot
167	SE	25	6	0	19	28	24	53	83
168	LMS	25	5	9	19	26	24	55	86
169	LMS	26·7	5	9	19½	26	25	52	88
170	LMS	26·7	5	9	19½	26	25	50	85
171	LNE	24·5	5	2	20	26	32	59	89
172	BR	26·7	5	8	18	28	26	53	87
173	LMS	25	5	8	16	26	25	57	92
174	SR	25	5	6	16½	28	30	57	91
175	GE	13·9	3	10	17	20	20	38	38
176	LMS	11·8	3	10	15½	20	15	33	33
177	GW	12·8	5	2	16	24	14	28	42
178	LBS	15·7	5	6	17	24	16	33	48
179	Met	21·4	5	9	19	26	19	39	77
180	NE	23	5	9	16½	26	23	40	87
181	MR	21·1	5	7	18½	26	20	53	73
182	SE	17·6	5	6	19½	26	21	52	71
183	NS	21	5	6	20	26	22	56	74
184	LNW	24	5	8	20	26	23	45	78
185	GC	21	5	7	20	26	24	54	86
186	NE	23	5	1	19	26	23	52	76
187	LSW	27	5	7	21	28	29	59	97
188	LBS	25·2	6	7½	21	26	21	71	89
189	CR	21	5	9	19½	26	21	55	92

* 1 Stephenson   1 Walschaerts.

H Super Grate	S_v mph	S_c mph	Y	Date of first	No in class	Class
2/2-6-4T						
8·1	35–70	52–73	PW	1917	1	790
10·7	43–86	52–73	PW	1927	125	Fowler
8·6	42–84	53–75	PW	1936	206	Stanier
8·6	42–84	53–75	PW	1945	277	Fairburn
11·6	26–52	47–64	PW	1945	100	9000 LNE L1
9·3	42–84	51–72	PW	1951	155	4
3/2-6-4T						
6·2	34–68	50–70	PW	1934	37	2500
11·4	35–70	42–59	PW	1931	15	W
2/0-4-0T						
—	12–24	29–40	FW	1913	5	B74 LNE Y4
—	13–26	33–45	FS	1932	5	ST
0-4-2T						
—	15–30	38–53	FS	1932	95	4800
—	15–30	41–57	FS	1910	1	79A
2/4-4-4T						
12·5	24–48	56–79	PW	1920	8	LNE H2
3/4-4-4T						
11·8	35–70	50–70	PS	1913	45	D
0-6-4T						
—	13–26	44–61	PS	1907	40	2000
13·3	18–36	42–59	PS	1913	5	J
12·3	17–34	48–67	PS	1916	16	114
4-6-2T						
10·4	22–44	52–73	PJ	1910	47	2665
8·5	21–42	44–61	PS	1911	21	9N LNE A5
—	16–32	42–58	PS	1909	10	W
2/4-6-2T						
9·4	20–40	46–65	PW	1921	5	H16
14	23–46	60–84	PW*	1910	2	J
10·2	18–36	51–71	PS	1917	12	944

Ref	Rly	G Grate Area (sq ft)	D Wheel Dia ft ins		d Cyl Dia ins	s Piston stroke ins	t Nom TE (1,000 lb)	Wt Ad tons	Tot
190	NE	23	4	7	$16\frac{1}{2}$	26	29	56	87
191	LNE	23	5	9	$16\frac{1}{2}$	26	23	53	87
192	FR	26	5	8	$19\frac{1}{2}$	26	21	55	93
193	LBS	26·7	6	$7\frac{1}{2}$	22	28	25	57	98
194	LTS	25	6	3	20	26	19	54	98
195	GS	30	6	0	22	26	27	54	99
196	LMS	29·6	6	3	$16\frac{1}{2}$	26	30	56	100
197	LNW	23·6	4	5	$20\frac{1}{2}$	24	28	62	72
198	GN	24·5	4	$7\frac{1}{2}$	20	26	28	66	79
199	LY	25·6	4	6	$21\frac{1}{2}$	26	34	70	86
200	LNW	23·6	4	5	$20\frac{1}{2}$	24	30	67	88
201	GW	20·6	4	$7\frac{1}{2}$	19	30	33	73	82
202	GW	20·6	4	$7\frac{1}{2}$	19	30	33	73	93
203	LSW	27	5	1	22	28	34	73	95
204	SR	18·6	4	8	16	28	30	72	72
205	GC	26·3	4	8	18	26	35	74	97
206	NE	23	4	7	18	26	35	52	85
207	GE	42	4	6	$18\frac{1}{2}$	24	39	80	80
208	LMS	44·5	5	3	$18\frac{1}{2}$	26	46	122	156
209	LNE	56	4	8	$18\frac{1}{2}$	26	73	144	178

H Super Grate	S_v mph	S_c mph	Y	Date of first	No in class	Class
3/4-6-2T						
—	17–34	33–46	PS	1910	20	Y
8·4	27–54	50–70	PS	1931	45	Rebuilt 4-4-4 LNE A8
4-6-4T						
—	24–48	52–72	PS	1921	6	115
2/4-6-4T						
14·3	21–42	54–75	PW	1914	7	L WT
12·8	24–48	66–92	PS	1912	8	2101
8·5	19–38	56–79	PW	1922	6	540
4/4-6-4T						
14·5	37–74	49–69	PW	1924	10	11110
0-8-2T						
—	10–20	35–48	FJ	1911	30	289
—	10–20	37–51	FS	1903	41	YT
—	9–18	42–58	FJ	1908	5	1501
0-8-4T						
15·2	17–34	39–55	PJ	1923	30	380
2/2-8-0T						
9·3	27–54	31–44	PS	1910	205	4200
2/2-8-2T						
9·3	27–54	31–44	PS	1934	55	7200
2/4-8-0T						
9·5	16–32	40–56	PW	1921	4	G16
3/0-8-0T						
—	22–44	26–36	PW	1930	8	Z
3/0-8-4T						
—	11–22	35–48	FS	1908	6	8H LNE S1
3/4-8-0T						
—	16–32	27–38	PS	1909	4	X
3/0-10-0WT						
—	11–22	45–63	FS	1903	1	Decapod
4/2-6 — 6-2						
11·2	23–46	48–67	PW	1927	33	Garratt
6/2-8 — 8-2						
11·5	25–50	38–53	PW	1925	1	Garratt

GRADED PERF
LOCOMOTIVES

Ref	Grade of power	Railway	Class of locomotive	R	No of loco	Ave Speed mph
1	26	LNE	A4 4-6-2(f)	119	4901	75.2
2		LMS	Reb. Scot(f)	62	6154	52.7
3	23	GW	2-6-0	76	5326	53.0
4		GW	Star 4-6-0	65	4042	55.5
5		GW	King 4-6-0	67	6022	59.4
6		LNW	George V 4-4-0	12	1595	61.9
7		LMS	Rebuilt Scot 4-6-0(f)	62	?	71.0
8		LNE	C1 4-4-2	107	4404	61.3
9		Caled	Cardean 4-6-0	36	903	44.0
10	22	GW	Castle 4-6-0	66	4074	61.5
11		GW	Saint 4-6-0	37	2942	59.0
12	21	GW	County 4-6-0(d)	41	1010	56.3
13		LNW	Claughton 4-6-0	68	1159	62.2
14		NE	Z 4-4-2	112	732	58.2
15		LMS	5 4-6-0	53	5020	58.3
16		LMS	Royal Scot 4-6-0	59	6131	64.5
17		Southern	School 4-4-0	28	932	58.7
18	20	GW	County 4-4-0(e)	25	3834	50.0
19		GN	1000 2-6-0	83	1007	51.0
20		LMS	Duchess 4-6-2(f)	128	6234	56.5
21		LNE	B17 4-6-0	63	2848	57.7
22	19	LNW	Prince 4-6-0	31	160	57.9
23		GE	Claud 4-4-0	18	1809	51.5
24		LMS	Princess 4-6-2	127	6200	69.5
25		LNE	A3 4-6-2	118	2746	60.0 (g)
26		LNE	P2 2-8-2(f)	132	2001	59.2
27		Southern	Nelson 4-6-0(f)	75	865	53.2
28		LNW	Benbow 4-4-0(h)	—	1941	54.0

ORMANCES OF
see page 142

Time (min)	Load (tons)	DHP	Date in RM	Route
20	730	2120	Oct 1940	Otterington–Poppleton J
10	515	1720	—	Axminster MP142–133¼ (k)
65	465	950	Feb 1934	Paddington–Ardley
76	525	1080	June 1924	Paddington–Savernake
175	575	1230	Sept 1933	Exeter–Paddington
138	410	910	Jan 1912	Willesden–Whitmore
65	515	1350	Mar 1954	Rugby–Willesden
75	585	1200	Oct 1936	Barkston–Chaloner Whin
18.5	390	1200	Nov 1936	Penrith–Shap Summit
169	530(c)	1030	July 1925	Paddington–Exeter
65	485	1090	Apr 1927	Reading–Badminton
78	495	1050	July 1948	Taunton–Savernake
152	435	1050	—	Euston–Crewe
37	545	1090	June 1912	Beningbrough–Croft
85	495	1050	Nov 1934	Euston–Rugby
143	470	1120	Dec 1934	Crewe–Willesden
44	510	1130	Oct 1939	Wimbledon–Worting J
46	330	760	May 1917	Hereford–Church Stretton
75	605	1000	Sept 1921	Peterborough–Potters Bar
33	610	1900	May 1939	Carnforth–Shap Summit
82	465	980	Dec 1939	Leicester–Amersham
74	465	840	July 1916	Rugby–Harrow
109	400	690	Nov 1911	Trowse–Ingrave
132	500	1380	Apr 1939	Crewe–Willesden
200	615	1170	Apr 1933	Newcastle–King's Cross
11	650	2020	Aug 1934	Essendine–Stoke Box
19.5	495	1360	Oct 1939	Eastleigh–Litchfield
86	480	715	Dec 1904	Rugby–Willesden

Ref	Grade of power	Railway	Class of locomotive	R	No of loco	Ave Speed mph
29	18	GE	1500 4-6-0	34	1566	55.0
30		LMS	5XP 4-6-0	61	5660	59.7
31		LNE	A1 4-6-2	116	4472	58.0
32		Southern	Arthur 4-6-0	55	768	57.2
33	17	Caled	140 4-4-0	—	140	45.8
34		LMS	Compound 4-4-0	26	913	49.0
35		LY	2-4-2T	149	1532	29.7
36	16	LNE	D49 4-4-0	27	249	41.6
37		Southern	MN 4-6-2(f)	124	21C4	61.3
38	15	BR	Britannia 4-6-2	114	70009	71.5
39	14	LNE	V2 2-6-2	129	60889	64.0
40		Southern	WC 4-6-2(f)	125	34006	35.6

(c) Reduced by slipping to 455 at Westbury and 390 at Taunton.
(d) Hawksworth 'County' 4-6-0.
(e) Churchward 'County' 4-4-0.
(f) Multiple-jet blast-pipe.
(g) For a total of 200 miles.
(h) Four-cylinder compound 4-4-0.
(j) Western end of tunnel.
(k) During 'locomotive exchanges' 1948.

Time (min)	Load (tons)	DHP	Date in RM	Route
55	415	870	Oct 1922	Stratford–Ardleigh
49	305	1060	Dec 1937	Carlisle–Aisgill
66	615	1290	Oct 1938	Peterborough–Potters Bar
73	460	950	May 1935	Salisbury–Honiton (*j*)
30	404	750	Nov 1905	Strawfrank Jc–Beattock S
45	375	880	Apr 1932	Dumfries–New Cumnock
10.9	250	675	Dec 1922	Stubbins J–Baxenden
24	435	810	—	Berwick–Grantshouse
46	575	1380	Mar 1949	Wilton–MP 133
43	470	1240	July 1951	Blisworth–Harrow
66	510	1060	Sept 1950	Wood Green–Fletton J
11	395	1110	—	Aylesbury–MP31½ (*k*)

COAL CONSUMPTION

IN THE following table, test values are quoted for the basically important ratio of coal burned per unit of work done in pulling the train. This figure omits to take account of the heat value of the coal per pound (this can vary more than 10 per cent between varieties of coal) and of the cost of coal per pound. The first defect could be avoided by quoting instead the ratio of useful work done to the thermal energy in the coal burned, but it is traditional not to do this probably because the ratio – of the order of 6 per cent – is so depressingly low.

This ratio also varies with the ratio of weight of train to weight of locomotive. Every locomotive burned infinite coal per drawbar-horsepower hour when it ran without a train because the drawbar horsepower was then zero.

The figure in the extreme right-hand column is the weight of coal required to make the locomotive produce two million foot-pounds of work at the drawbar. This is one 'drawbar-horsepower hour'.

COAL CONSUMPTION OF SOME SUPERHEATED STEAM
LOCOMOTIVES

Date of first engine	Rly		Class	R*	$\dfrac{lb}{dhp\ hr}$
1911	GN	2/4-4-2	1452	107	5·1
1911	LNW	4-6-0	'Prince'	31	5·1
1911	NE	3/4-4-2	Z	112	4·5
1912	NB	2/4-4-2	H	111	4·1
1920	NE	3/0-8-0	T3	97	4·4

Date of first engine	Rly	Class		R*	lb / dhp hr
1922	MR	3C/4-4-0	1000	26	4·1
1922	LY	4/4-6-0	Rebuilt	72	4·8
1922	LY	do. with 6-ring valves		72	4·0
1923	GW	4/4-6-0	Castle	66	2·8
1926	LMS	2/2-6-0	Horwich	82	3·4
1927	LMS	3/4-6-0	Royal Scot	59	3·3
1927	LNE	3/4-6-2	A1 and A3	116/8	3·1
1930	LMS	0-8-0	Fowler	93	2·8
1931	LMS	3/4-6-0	Baby Scot	60	3·1
1933	LMS	4/4-6-2	Princess	127	3·0
1937	LMS	4/4-6-2	Duchess	128	2·9
		1948 Exchanges			
1927	GW	4/4-6-0	King	67	3·6
1928	GW	2/4-6-0	Hall	38	4·0
1934	LMS	2/4-6-0	Class 5	53	3·5
1935	LNE	3/4-6-2	A4	119	3·1
1937	LMS	4/4-6-2	Duchess	128	3·1
1941	SR	3/4-6-2	M't Navy	124	3·6
1942	LNE	2/4-6-0	B1	54	3·6
1943	LMS	3/4-6-0	Rebuilt Scot	62	3·4
1946	SR	3/4-6-2	West Country	125	4·2

* Reference number in Appendix 2.

AVERAGE MILEAGE BETWEEN SUCCESSIVE GENERAL REPAIRS

IT MUST be pointed out that mileage is only an approximate measure of utility because, for example, a mile up 1 in 200 at 60 mph with 600 tons is different from a mile on the level at 20 mph with 100 tons. But for large numbers of locomotives it was hardly practicable to go into detail beyond mileage. Below are given some typical figures from Bib. 28.

Region	R*	Thousands of miles		Class
LM	128	73	4/4-6-2	Coronation
	62	70	3/4-6-0	Rebuilt Scot
	53	57	2/4-6-0	Class 5
	53	97	2/4-6-0	Note (a)
	102	50	2/2-8-0	Class 8F
E/NE	123	93	3/4-6-2	Peppercorn A1
	121	86	3/4-6-2	Peppercorn A2
	118	84	3/4-6-2	Gresley A3
	119	87	3/4-6-2	Gresley A4
	54	78	2/4-6-0	B1
	103	56	2/2-8-0	O1
	129	78	3/2-6-2	V2
Western	67	79	4/4-6-0	King
	66	87	4/4-6-0	Castle
	38	88	2/4-6-0	Hall
	41	88	2/4-6-0	County
	98	87	2/2-8-0	2800

| | | Thousands | | |
Region	R*	of miles		Class
Southern	124	76	3/4-6-2	Merchant Navy
	125	75	3/4-6-2	West Country
	75	82	4/4-6-0	Lord Nelson
	55	71	2/4-6-0	King Arthur
	28	70	3/4-4-0	School

* Reference number in Appendix 2.

(*a*) Class 5 with manganese steel liners for axleboxes.

BIBLIOGRAPHY

(*RM* denotes *Railway Magazine*)

1. Tuplin, W. A., 1953. 'Some questions about the steam locomotive', *Journal Inst. Loco. Engineers*, No 236.
2. *The locomotives of the Great Western Railway*, Part 5, Railway Correspondence and Travel Society.
3. *RM* 1923. Nov, p 391.
4. *Railway Observer* 1963. Dec, p. 385.
5. Tuplin, W. A., 1950. 'Locomotive cylinder power', *The Engineer*, Feb. 10th/17th, pp 171–214.
6. *Modern Railways* 1963. April, p 263.
7. *RM* 1922. Dec, p 429.
8. Mason, E., 1954. *Lancashire & Yorkshire Railway* (Ian Allan), p 79.
9. Ell, S. O., 1953. 'Developments in Locomotive Testing', *Journal Inst. Loco. Engineers*, No 235, Fig 9, Fig 11.
10. Cox, E. S., 1946. 'A modern locomotive history', *Journal Inst. Loco. Engineers*, No 190, p 136.
11. Cox, E. S., 1967. *Chronicles of Steam*, p 115 (Ian Allan)
12. Gresley, H. N., 1928. 'Report on comparative tests on LNE "Pacifics"', *The Engineer*, June 15th, p 668.
13. Spencer, B., 1947. 'Development of LNE locomotive design', *Journal Inst. Loco. Enginneers*, No 197, p 223. Cox, E. S., ibid, p 214.
14. Stanier, W. A., 1941. 'Position of the locomotive in mechanical engineering', *Proc. I. Mech. E.*, Vol 146, No 2, p 56.
15. *RM* 1932. Oct, p 245.
16. *RM* 1932. Aug, p 99.

17. *RM* 1935. Oct, p 248.
18. *RM* 1923. July, p 21.
19. *RM* 1924. Dec, p 455.
20. *RM* 1922. July, p 38.
21. *RM* 1922. Oct, p 265.
22. *RM* 1912. June, p 497.
23. *RM* 1934. Sept, p 169.
24. *RM* 1932. April, p 305.
25. *RM* 1937. Nov, p 338.
26. Bib. 1, p 650.
27. Bib. 1, p 652.
28. Bond, R. C., 1953. 'Organization and control of loco-
    motive repairs', *Journal Inst. Loco. Engineers*, No 232,
    p 183.
29. Tuplin, W. A., 1964. 'An ultimate steam locomotive'.
    The Engineer, Aug 28th, p 330.
30. *Modern Railways* 1963. Dec, p 422.
31. *RM* 1922. Nov, p 349.
32. Tuplin, W. A., 1955. 'Loads in locomotive coupling-
    rods', *The Engineer*, Sept 2nd, p 327.
33. Langley, C. A., 1960. Ministry of Transport Railway
    accident report, April 19th (Settle).
34. *RM* 1936. Sept, p 168.
35. *RM* 1939. Oct, p 248.
36. *RM* 1937. Jan, p 62.
37. Cox, E. S., 1966. *British Railways Standard Locomotives*
    (Ian Allan).
38. Holcroft, H., 1962. *Locomotive Adventure*, Vol I (Ian
    Allan), pp 68, 91.
39. Holcroft, H., 1918. *The Engineer*, August 2nd, p 96.

GENERAL INDEX

INDEX OF CLASSES OF LOCOMOTIVES

GREAT CENTRAL

GREAT EASTERN

NORTH BRITISH

LONDON & SOUTH WESTERN

SOUTH EASTERN & CHATHAM

INDEX OF INDIVIDUAL LOCOMOTIVES

* Liverpool & Manchester Railway (1830).

INDEX OF PEOPLE

INDEX OF PLACES

THE MOST SOUGHT AFTER SERIES IN THE '70'S

These superb David & Charles titles are now available in PAN, for connoisseurs, enthusiasts, tourists and everyone looking for a deeper appreciation of Britain than can be found in routine guide books.

LNER STEAM   O. S. Nock   50p
A masterly account with superb photographs showing every aspect of steam locomotive design and operation on the LNER.

THE SAILOR'S WORLD   T. A. Hampton   35p
A guide to ships, harbours and customs of the sea. 'Will be of immense value' – PORT OF LONDON AUTHORITY. Illustrated.

OLD DEVON   W. G. Hoskins   45p
'As perfect an account of the social, agricultural and industrial grassroots as one could hope to find' – THE FIELD. Illustrated.

INTRODUCTION TO INN SIGNS   Eric R. Delderfield   35p
This beautifully illustrated and fascinating guide will delight everyone who loves the British pub. Illustrated.

THE CANAL AGE   Charles Hadfield   50p
A delightful look at the waterways of Britain, Europe and North America from 1760 to 1850. Illustrated.

BUYING ANTIQUES   A. W. Coysh and J. King   45p
An invaluable guide to buying antiques for pleasure or profit. 'Packed with useful information' – QUEEN MAGAZINE. Illustrated.

RAILWAY ADVENTURE   L. T. C. Rolt   35p
The remarkable story of the Talyllyn Railway from inception to the days when a band of local enthusiasts took over its running. Illustrated.

A SELECTION OF POPULAR READING IN PAN

FICTION

SILENCE ON MONTE SOLE	Jack Olsen	35p
COLONEL SUN A new James Bond novel by		
	Robert Markham	25p
THE LOOKING-GLASS WAR	John le Carré	25p
THE FAME GAME	Rona Jaffe	40p
CATHERINE AND A TIME FOR LOVE		
	Julietta Benzoni	35p
THE ASCENT OF DI3	Andrew Garve	25p
THE FAR SANDS	Andrew Garve	25p
AIRPORT	Arthur Hailey	37½p
REQUIEM FOR A WREN	Nevil Shute	30p
SYLVESTER	Georgette Heyer	30p
ROSEMARY'S BABY	Ira Levin	25p
HEIR TO FALCONHURST	Lance Horner	40p
THE MURDER IN THE TOWER	Jean Plaidy	30p
GAY LORD ROBERT	Jean Plaidy	30p
A CASE OF NEED	Jeffery Hudson	35p
THE ROSE AND THE SWORD	Sandra Paretti	40p

NON-FICTION

THE SOMERSET & DORSET RAILWAY (illus.)		
	Robin Atthill	35p
THE WEST HIGHLAND RAILWAY (illus.)		
	John Thomas	35p
MY BEAVER COLONY (illus.) .	Lars Wilsson	25p
THE PETER PRINCIPLE	Dr. Laurence J. Peter	
	and Raymond Hull	30p
THE ROOTS OF HEALTH	Leon Petulengro	20p

These and other advertised PAN Books are obtainable from all booksellers and newsagents. If you have any difficulty please send purchase price plus 5p postage to P.O. Box 11, Falmouth, Cornwall.

While every effort is made to keep prices low, it is sometimes necessary to increase prices at short notice. PAN Books reserve the right to show new retail prices on covers which may differ from these previously advertised in the text or elsewhere.